i
be
by
pt
la.

Roddy Martine was born in Kuching, Sarawak, the land of the Dyaks on the island of Borneo, and he therefore was exposed to the world of the supernatural at an early age. Of Scottish parentage, he has lived for most of his life in Edinburgh where, after leaving school, he edited a number of Scottish interest magazines before reinventing himself as a newspaper columnist, broadcaster and social commentator. He remains a contributing editor to *Scotland* magazine, and is the editor of *The Keeper*, the magazine of The Keepers of the Quaich, an exclusive society formed within the Scotch whisky industry to promote and celebrate its products. He has written over twenty non-fiction works.

SUPERNATURAL SCOTLAND

Roddy Martine has embarked upon a personal odyssey in search of the inexplicable and bizarre in every corner of Scotland. Amongst the dozens of incidents recorded, he tells of the hostile presence at the Goblin Ha' — a vaulted chamber below the ruins of Yester Castle — which exerted enormous pressure on his chest and legs, forcing him backwards. He investigates the mystery surrounding the burial of the murdered secretary of Mary, Queen of Scots, and meets His Grace James IV, King of Scots, reborn as the playwright A. J. Stewart. There are many other tales of ghosts and poltergeists, second sight, psychic phenomena, reincarnation, and the small people.

RODDY MARTINE

SUPERNATURAL SCOTLAND

Complete and Unabridged

ULVERSCROFT
Leicester

First published in Great Britain in 2003 by
Robert Hale Limited
London

First Large Print Edition
published 2004
by arrangement with
Robert Hale Limited
London

Photographic Credits
Photographers International: 12.
National Galleries of Scotland: 13.
All other photographs are from the author's collection.

British Library CIP Data

Martine, Roddy, *1946 –*
    Supernatural Scotland.—Large print ed.—
    Ulverscroft large print series: non-fiction
    1. Supernatural—Scotland
    2. Ghosts—Scotland
    3. Large type books
    I. Title
    133.1′09411

    ISBN 1–84395–405–2

Published by
F. A. Thorpe (Publishing)
Anstey, Leicestershire

Set by Words & Graphics Ltd.
Anstey, Leicestershire
Printed and bound in Great Britain by
T. J. International Ltd., Padstow, Cornwall

This book is printed on acid-free paper

To Christian Broun Lindsay,who was
such a source of encouragement and
enthusiasm to the author when
writing this book

Contents

Acknowledgements

From the very beginning *Supernatural Scotland* has been both a challenging and stimulating project, and to bring so much information together from so many sources would not have been possible had it not been for the help of the following: Kate Anderson; Audley Archdale; Mary Armour; John Beaton; Neil Blackburn; Laurence, Jenny, Charles and Amelia Blair Oliphant; Marian Bowles; Beatrice, Christian, Ludovic and Frances Broun Lindsay; David Burns; Lindy Cameron; Jacqueline Coia; Fiona Colton; Fidelma Cook; Jonny and Tuggy Delap; Colette Douglas Home; Ian Easton; Philippa Grant; Stewart Grant; John Gray; Nicholas Groves Raines; Lady Marioth Hay; Lorraine and Katherine Hedges; Carol Hogel; James Hunter-Blair; David Ingram; James and Carolle Irvine Robertson; Stuart B. Kelly; Dr Elspeth King; Alistair and Alanna Knight; Rory and Kirsty Knight Bruce; Ian Landles; Mark Leishman; Angus Lockhart; Hugh Lockhart; Swein MacDonald; Sheena McDonald; Catriona McGee; Archie Mackenzie; Dr Finlay MacLeod; William McNair;

Zandra Macpherson; Tommy MacRae; David Marriott; Irene Martine; Roy Miller; Bridget Miller-Mundy; Brendan Murphy; Alasdair Morrison, MSP; Adam Nicolson; Sir Iain Noble, Bt; Lady Noble; Sheila Pitcairn; Nicholas Radcliffe; Douglas Rae; The Revd Charles Robertson; Joan Robertson; Norrie Rowan; John Salkeld; Elizabeth Salvesen; Peter Samson; Pavel Satny; Sandy Scott; Adrian Shaw; Dr Michael Shea; A. J. Stewart; Sya Simpson; Suki Urquhart; Jamie Walker; Felix Wilson; Theresa Wilson; Janet Wotherspoon.

The author would particularly like to thank A. J. Stewart for permission to quote from her work, and the Lockhart Family for allowing him to make use of the material of J. G. Lockhart.

Introduction

Man, precariously perched on this rotating scrap-heap, yet so much master of it that he could mould it to his transient uses and, while struggling to live, could entertain thoughts and dreams beyond the bounds of time and space! Man so weak and yet so great, this chief handiwork of the Power that had hung the stars in the firmament!

John Buchan *Sick Heart River*

The writing of this book has posed the author with an intriguing adventure into territories he has hitherto consciously avoided. None of us likes to open ourselves up to ridicule. Once we start to explore the realms of the inexplicable, all kinds of extraordinary, self-indulgent ideas surface. Education instructs us to be curious, but within logical boundaries. Ignorance and fear hold us back to the extent that we can joke about it. Religions, while steeped in their own miracles, discourage independent investigation. Certain faiths go so far as to forbid it unequivocally.

In an age when technological discovery is racing ahead faster than we can keep up with it, we prefer our day-to-day activities to be ordered and logical. The majority of us have long ago lost touch with the discerning world of our ancestors where glimpses of another time were not considered to be unusual.

As society becomes increasingly urbanized, organized and sanitized, we take much of what is about us for granted. If four hundred years ago somebody had claimed that it was possible to speak to people on the other side of the world by telephone or send messages on the internet, fly to the moon, see in the dark, or watch moving images on a silver screen, they would at best have been placed in an asylum, or at worst, burned for witchcraft.

The further we are removed from our primal origins, the less we have become aware of the dimension we inhabit. Often it is only the children among us who unquestioningly accept the metaphysical simply because the rest of us have lost our ability to do so. Why are the new religions so afraid of the old religions? Why is it that the more we distance ourselves from the pagan beliefs of our ancestors, the greater becomes our inability to relate to the possibilities of an afterlife?

During their lifetimes, science fiction writers such as Jules Verne and H. G. Wells wrote about the future and were celebrated for the absurdity of their inventiveness, but virtually everything they foresaw has come to pass.

The supernatural is a global subject, and by concentrating on Scotland with its limited land mass, its dark and turbulent history and climatic landscape, a pattern emerges which can be translated to anywhere at any time. For this book, the most unlikely people have come forward with their stories. As the body of evidence accumulates, even the most dismissive debunker has ultimately to concede that there must surely be more to the world of the occult than mere fantasy.

Without entering into scientific debate, we can reflect that more often than not artists, musicians and writers have no idea where their ideas come from. Possibly they are suggestible, influenced by those they live with, their surroundings, and what takes place in their lives, but this does not fully explain how so much information accumulates in the subconscious. We call it 'The Muse', the inspiration that arrives after writer's block.

But what exactly is it that mobilizes the creativity that exists within every one of us to some degree or another? The human mind, with the senses that it employs when it chooses, is the most astonishing phenomenon of all.

Sometimes the words, the sounds and the brush strokes flow as if some hidden force is driving them, on occasion using an unfamiliar vocabulary or an unprecedented style. To this end, supernatural occurrences — ghosts of the past, poltergeists, psychic phenomena, second sight, reincarnation and transition from one form to another — are all part of the human condition. The more our knowledge of the known world increases alongside the technology we devise to analyze it, the more questions there are to be asked and the more uncertain we become.

And I, for one, am thankful for this. Without mystery or illusion, life would soon become a bleak and unchallenging existence. Throughout this book I have endeavoured to avoid being judgemental. Sometimes the episodes are comic; more often than not they are sad, and sometimes even tragic. By bringing them to light, unexplained incidents can lead to a better understanding of the uncertainties of the mortal world as a whole. Sometimes it is best not to dig too deeply.

In certain cases, at their own request, it has been necessary to change, or at least disguise, the names of individuals to prevent them from being compromised. In general, however, those who have furnished me with the bulk of personal anecdote have stepped forward willingly and without conditions, for which I would like to thank them. As the body of material has grown in volume, so has the realization that there is far more to our day-to-day existence on this earth than the majority of us are aware of, or prepared to admit. In the realms of the supernatural, who is to say what is real and what is not? Ultimately, readers must decide for themselves.

1

The Rational Mind

From ghoulies and ghosties and long
    leggety beasties
And things that go bump in the night,
Good Lord deliver us.

                    Old Scottish prayer

At a dinner party in Northern Spain, I found myself seated beside an Italian lady architect from Florence. 'Ah, Scotland,' she sighed gently, when she learned where I was from. 'Castles and ghosts.'

'Why do you say that?' I asked, wondering why not tartan, Scotch whisky, Robert Burns or bagpipes?

'Because that is what everybody knows about Scotland,' she replied with that far away look people have in their eyes when their imagination is aroused. 'Castles and ghosts.'

This made me ponder on my own experiences of the supernatural in Scotland. Haunting is universal. Every country has its own stories of phantoms and psychic phenomena, but Scotland is somehow special. It might have something to do with the weather, the rain and the mist and the wind. It certainly has a lot to do with the light and the landscape. Ghosts are not usually associated with sunlight. Multifarious shades of grey offset by greens and browns and purples, the sudden shaft of silver on the surface of remote lochans, the sense of isolation that pervades much of the countryside, the ink black nights and the long winters, all of these normalities influence our objectivity. Then there is the architecture, from the rubbled remains of Highland shielings and fortified keeps and castles to the cobbled streets and more recent, modernist pretensions of our inner cities.

In such a small country densely allocated with historic sites against a violent and colourful history, the ghosts of our past are more often than not laughably dismissed or taken for granted. Increasingly we shrug them off as nonsense, dismissing them as indulgent aberration. In an age of high technology it is hard to accommodate the inexplicable.

Yet given awareness, and a willingness to believe that there are dimensions into which science has failed to penetrate, anything is possible. In *The Roots of Coincidence*,

Arthur Koestler observed that it has become a common belief that in some instances time flows backwards. Furthermore, ghosts are thought to materialize by drawing heat-energy from their surroundings, hence the sudden chill so often noticed when an apparition materializes. Although I personally still find it hard to accept that parallel worlds exist, there have certainly been occurrences in my life that I am at a total loss to explain.

Probably the first example I can draw upon took place in 1968, when my sister Patty and I volunteered as weekend guides at Yester House, near Gifford in East Lothian.

Yester House is an architectural master-piece created by the Adam family of architects on the edge of the Lammermuir Hills. For centuries it was the seat of the Marquesses of Tweeddale until 1972 when it was bought by the Italian impresario Gian Carlo Menotti.

In 1968, however, it was still lived in by Marjorie, widow of the eleventh Marquess, and it was her bold initiative to open the doors to the public between June and October, recruiting family and friends to help out.

The recollections of one of the recruits, Lady Marioth Hay, sister of the twelfth Marquess, are outlined later in this book, but

3

for my part I found myself showing groups of visitors the main staircase and ballroom, explaining the decorative features and generally outlining the history of the family. Around 8,000 people visited Yester that summer, and often during the mid-afternoon round, an audible tap-tapping could be heard coming from a corridor that ran parallel to the far side of the ballroom.

To begin with I thought that it must simply be somebody wearing high-heeled shoes who had got lost, and on a couple of occasions I opened the door into the passage to see who it was. There was nobody there, and when I mentioned it to Marjorie Tweeddale she smiled. 'It's my mother-in-law with her stick,' she said. 'She never went out much before she died and liked to take her exercise walking up and down that corridor. She would also bang on the floor when she wanted attention.'

From then on, whenever I heard the tapping, I would impress the tour party by telling them what it was. It made a good story, but I only thought of it as a bit of fun. Then twenty-five years later I went to visit Maestro Menotti and as we sat down to lunch I casually asked him how he was getting on with the old lady in the corridor. He froze on the spot and looking accusingly across the table towards his son Chips said, 'Did you hear what he said?'

Apparently old Lady Tweeddale had been making such a racket since the Menottis had moved into the house that Gian Carlo had eventually brought in a priest to exorcise her.

My other Yester 'experience' concerns the Goblin Ha', the astonishing 37 feet vaulted chamber which sits below the ruins of Yester Castle in dense woodland a mile or so from the modern day palatial mansion. The local legend that the red sandstone castle's thirteenth century builder Hugo de Gifford, had been in league with the Devil is immortalized in The Host's Tale of Sir Walter Scott's *Marmion*. Allegedly this Prince of Darkness employed goblins, yet a more rational explanation, perhaps, is that he had imported black slaves from the Africas, something nobody would have hitherto seen in Scotland.

Hugo de Gifford features elsewhere in this book, but for the present anecdote suffice it to say that what he achieved at Yester Castle was by the standards of the day, and even now, profoundly impressive despite it being virtually inaccessible. Time has sadly not favoured it well, but I have to admit that it remains both the most sinister and the most fascinating place I have ever known.

The thickly overgrown ruins sit on a ridge above the Hopes Water, which gives the appearance of encircling them, and the entrance to the vaulted chamber, supported by its elegant arches, is now sealed off. Thirty-five years ago, however, the little postern gate was unlocked and during the summer months, the Marquess's granddaughter, Vicky Fletcher, and I often went there for picnics accompanied by her pug Bear.

Naturally I ventured down the steps into the Goblin Ha' many times, but on one occasion I took a torch with me intending to explore a passage on the far side that I had been told led to a shallow well fed by an underground spring. Legend has it that the dressed sandstone blocks which seal off the foot of the tunnel also conceal the entrance to an inner sanctum wherein spirits of the underworld are gathered to await patiently the summons of their Master. Vicky and Bear followed me. The passage was narrow and steep and we moved in a single file until suddenly the light from my torch went out. This puzzled me since the batteries were new, but I did not have any time to think about it. A deathly coldness surrounded us, seeping into me, and I began to experience an astonishingly hostile pressure on my chest and legs, forcing me backwards. It was as if several large hands were shoving at me, pushing me away from them. I have to admit that I was terrified.

'Go back, Vicky!' I shouted. We were both in a state of panic, and Bear dashed ahead of us through the entrance to the hall and into the bright sunlight outside where he stood shivering. When I looked at my torch the light had come back on again. Around us the woodland sparkled in the sunshine. Everything was calm and unthreatening, but whatever it was in that passageway leading to goodness knows what, it certainly had not wanted us there.

When I talked about this afterwards I was told that others, including Marioth Hay's son Eddie Trotter, and the late Betty Sitwell, from Belmont at Coldstream, another family member, had had similar experiences while exploring the same passageway. In Betty's case, the pressure had come from behind her, once again a terrible, chilling coldness, but this time there was the sensation that someone or something was grasping to catch her hand.

I returned to Yester Castle and ventured into the Goblin Ha' on many occasions after that until the Ministry of Works finally put padlocks on the wrought iron gates. But I never went near that passageway again.

Another equally puzzling series of incidents, although infinitely less alarming, took place when I was in my early twenties and living in the second floor flat of a tenement in the West End of Edinburgh. Douglas Crescent remains one of those quiet residential streets thrown up on the outskirts of Edinburgh's central Georgian New Town during the late Victorian era. In the late 1970s, it was largely inhabited by retired gentlefolk; in the majority widows and spinsters, then as now with a predilection for lace curtains. As had been the practice throughout the building of the New Town, residential properties occupying three floors and a basement featured to the centre of the crescent, while the houses at either end were split into flats above the ground level.

I was starting out on my career, single in status, sharing the flat with a couple of friends of my own age and, in retrospect, the comings and goings of our circle of acquaintances must have provided a rich circus of entertainment for the disapproving neighbours. Those were happy, indulgent days, and life in the attic flat with its large rooms overlooking a garden to the back, and communal gardens beside the Water of Leith to the front, became one long party with a constant stream of visitors staying overnight.

And this was when the small boy in the striped velvet jacket emerged, always after we had been entertaining. To begin with, I thought it was the consequence of a cocktail of whisky, red Bordeaux and kümmell, the lethal after-dinner kick we all indulged in at the time. That first night I awoke around 4 a.m. from a fitful sleep to find him standing beside my bed and staring intently at me. I remember shouting out 'Who are you?' then feeling fairly stupid when he disappeared.

The following morning, knowing that I would be ridiculed, I said nothing. Soon afterwards I forgot all about the small boy in the striped velvet jacket. Then Rebecca came to stay.

Rebecca was in publishing and walking out with a friend of mine. It was during the three weeks of the Edinburgh Festival of 1979, and she had come to help out in the Festival press office. Rupert, her boy friend, was in London, so she occupied the guest bedroom alone, and on the second morning of her stay appeared at the breakfast table ashen faced.

'I didn't sleep a wink last night,' she said. 'There was someone in my room. He was watching me, a small boy with a pale face.'

'About four foot tall?' I said casually.

She nodded.

'Shoulder length fair hair and wearing a striped velvet jacket?'

A year later I saw him again, then a married couple from Aberdeenshire who were staying overnight had a similar experience. A few weeks later another visitor saw him. Each time the description was the same. None of these individuals had previously met with each other, and I had certainly never spoken about what I had seen to any of them. In retrospect, however, they all agreed that he seemed a friendly ghost, that none of us had felt threatened by him and that we had only been distressed by the terrible sense of loneliness we experienced when he vanished.

Eventually I decided I had to try to find out who he was. An investigation of the title deeds proved fruitless. The property had changed ownership several times between 1900 and 1930 and the names revealed very little about the occupants. Then by pure coincidence I was travelling from Edinburgh to Glasgow on a train and found myself in a conversation with an elderly lady, commiserating with one another when our carriage came to an abrupt halt and sat motionless for over half an hour somewhere east of Falkirk.

'Have you far to go,' she asked.

'Haymarket,' I told her.

'Oh, whereabouts?'

When I told her where I lived she looked astonished. 'My mother was born in that house,' she told me. 'It belonged to my grandparents, but when my uncle died of leukaemia when he was twelve years old they couldn't bear to be there any more, so they moved.'

'When was that?' I asked.

'Some time early in the century,' she said. 'At any rate before the First World War, because my grandfather was killed at the Somme.'

'Do you remember your uncle's name?'

'Edward Seton,' she said directly.

Over a year passed before I saw Edward Seton again. Instead of shouting at him this time, I spoke his name out loud. For a second the image appeared to grow stronger and then it was gone.

I sold the flat in 1985 and failed to mention the permanent resident to the new occupiers. Besides, Edward Seton meant no harm. I think he was just curious to know who was living there with him. I hope they are kind to him.

2

The Legacy of Hugo de Gifford

A wiser never, at the hour
Of midnight, spoke the word of power;
The same, whom ancient records call
The founder of the Goblin-Hall.
I would, Sir Knight, your longer stay
Gave you that cavern to survey.
Of lofty roof and ample size,
Beneath the castle deep it lies:
To hew the living rock profound,
The floor to pave, the arch to round,
There never toil'd a mortal arm —

Sir Walter Scott, *Marmion XIX*,
'The Host's Tale'

On the basis of my known paternal ancestors
having emerged during the mid-fourteenth
century in and around the market town of
Haddington, on Scotland's south-east coast, I
decided that East Lothian would be as good a
place as any to begin my research. Not that I
had any intention of calling upon my
forebears for help, but consciously or

unconsciously, places of origin, the provenance from whence one's people came, do have a way of exercising an irrational pull.

Moreover, over a century ago my relative John Martine, grandson of a provost of the burgh, in his *Reminiscences and Notices of the Parishes of the County of Haddington* made frequent reference to the widespread incidence of ghostly visitations and the cult of witchcraft. A story he touched upon, and one that in the light of my personal experiences at Yester Castle particularly intrigued me, was the fable of the Colstoun Pear which I knew still to be in the possession of the Broun Lindsay family, owners of Colstoun House. Once again, their ancestor was that twelfth or thirteenth lord of the underworld, Sir Hugo de Gifford.

Gifford had two daughters, the elder of whom inherited his estates, but we are not concerned with her. It is her younger sister who is of interest, for she married the then Broun laird at the de Gifford family kirk. Sir Hugo had no dowry for his younger daughter, but outside the kirk there was a pear tree, and on leaving the kirk he stopped and plucked a pear which he gave to the newly weds with the promise that so long as it remained unharmed, no ill would befall the family.

In the late sixteenth century, Sir George Broun of Colstoun, second baronet, married Lady Elizabeth Mackenzie, daughter of the first Earl of Cromartie. There are two variations on the story of what then took place.

The first is that Lady Elizabeth was pregnant and asked to see the pear, whereupon she promptly bit it. The second is that she had a dream about the pear, that it was harmed, and so asked to see it. When she saw that it was in good condition, she took a bite of it.

Whichever version is correct, the repercussions were significant. Her husband, who was a gambler, incurred enormous debts and was forced to sell Colstoun. His younger brother Robert, who had married Margaret Bannatyne, the heiress to Newhall in Midlothian, then sold his wife's estate and bought Colstoun from his brother.

Robert was a member of the Scottish Parliament, and one night in the early 1700s he was returning from a late sitting of the House accompanied by his wife, two sons and daughter. The Colstoun Water was in spate, and the coach driver missed the ford and as a result, Robert and his two sons were drowned. His wife and daughter were saved by floating in the river courtesy of the air trapped in their crinolines.

Thus came to pass the curse of the pear. Between Robert Broun and his descendant James Andrew, tenth Earl and first Marquess of Dalhousie, there were no male heirs, and between the Marquis and the late Colin Broun Lindsay of Colstoun, there have been no male heirs.

The bloodline, nevertheless, survived. With Colstoun having been entailed during the lifetime of Robert Broun, the estate passed for several generations through the female line, with each heiress taking the name of Broun. The pear, as one might expect, has been kept safely under lock and key and is revered to this day as a priceless family treasure.

There are other examples of the reach of Hugo de Gifford across the millennium. It is said that when he heard that hostile armies were encroaching upon him from north and south, he made a pact with the Devil, promising sanctuary to his followers for eternity if they saved his castle. Within hours the enemy had dispersed, but woe betide anyone who seeks to substantiate this claim, especially his descendants. In 1800, the Earl of Gifford who was digging close to Yester Castle in the woods met his end when a beech tree fell upon him. As recently as 1970, a workman employed on restoration work on the ruins suffered a similar fate.

Marioth Hay, who lives at Gifford, often experienced psychic sensations when we guided together at Yester House. One day while driving home she came across a Canadian who had recently bought a house in the village and whose car had broken down. 'I must remember to take my metal detector out of the boot,' he told her. 'I've been up at the castle looking for treasure.' Two days later the postman informed Marioth that her passenger had died of a heart attack.

Another curious relic with debatable powers is the Lee Penny which remains the property of the Lockhart family who live in Lanarkshire.

In the fourteenth century, Sir Symon Lockhard, a young Border knight, was entrusted with the key to the silver box which contained the heart of Robert the Bruce, whose dying wish had been that it be taken to the Holy Land on a crusade. Bruce had wanted to atone for the murder of his cousin John Comyn in 1306.

Alas, the casket got no further than Spain where the carriers found themselves embroiled in the conflict between Alphonso,

King of Castile and Leon, and the Saracen army.

The story of what befell the 'good' Sir James Douglas, leader of the expedition is well known: in the ensuing confrontation, Douglas was killed having hurled the casket into the fray. Fortunately, it was retrieved by Sir William Keith and brought back to Scotland, where it was interred at Melrose Abbey.

In the meantime, Keith's side-kick, Sir Symon, had at some stage taken prisoner a wealthy Emir whose mother eventually arrived at the Christian camp to beg for his release. In the introduction to *The Talisman*, Sir Walter Scott relates that Lockhard agreed to a ransom, and the lady then produced the necessary coinage from a large embroidered purse.

In the course of handing over the money, however, a pebble inserted in a coin fell to the ground. Lockhard, noticing the lady's haste to retrieve it, said: 'I will not consent to grant your son's liberty, unless that amulet be added to his ransom.'

Amazingly, the lady not only agreed, but explained how the stone should be used, insisting that when dipped in water it possessed magical powers. According to Lockhart family tradition (the name was changed by a later generation to honour their ancestor's calling as keeper of the casket key, which incidentally he lost), the lady also revealed that the stone 'cures all diseases in cattle, and the bite of a mad dog both in man and beast.'

The process by which such miracles could be achieved was simple. The stone should be dipped three times and swirled round once in water, and this given to the diseased cattle to drink, or in the case of a dog bite, employed as a lotion to the wound. No money must pass hands and no words must be spoken during the ritual.

Some years ago I had the privilege of inspecting the Lee Penny. The stone itself, no more than a pebble in size, is of a dull deep crimson translucent colour and heart-shaped. It is embedded in the centre of a silver coin upon which the lettering is worn, and therefore indecipherable. The coin appears to be either an old shilling or a groat, which despite Sir Walter's assertion that it is 'Lower Empire', indicates that the stone was set into it long after it was brought home.

During the seventeenth century, when there was an outbreak of what would nowadays be known as foot and mouth disease in East Lothian, farming folk begged for the use of the penny. Instead they were given flagons of water into which it had been dipped three times and swirled, and such was the success rate, apparently, that Isobel Young of East Barns, who had accompanied the delegation, was later put on trial and subsequently burnt for witchcraft.

But that is by no means the end of the saga. The Talisman was again used in the reign of Charles I, and during the eighteenth and nineteenth centuries, when latterly bottles of water in which it had been dipped were hung from the rafters of every byre in Lanarkshire.

For many years, the Lockharts obliged the superstition of their neighbours by placing the penny in a bowl of water when they were the occupants at Lee Castle, near Carnwath. As late as the twentieth century, a Thomas Reid, who delivered a paper on the subject to the Society of Antiquaries of Scotland spoke of tasting the water in which the penny had been dipped three times and swirled, and said that it had a 'perceptibly peculiar flavour.' Stories circulated about cattle being miraculously cleansed and a man bitten by a mad horse being saved by it during an outbreak of rabies.

In his book *Curses, Lucks and Talismans,* J.G. Lockhart records an incident that took place a few years before the First World War.

The story is given without comment and exactly as it was related by someone staying in the house at the time. Sir Simon was entertaining a shooting party at Lee, and among the guests was a relative of the present Lord Hamilton of Dalzell. At luncheon on the moors it was discovered that, as so often happens, everything had been remembered except the small and necessary implement that opens soda-water bottles. Sir Simon tried to use his pocket knife, while Lord Hamilton's relative held the bottle, and in the struggle the knife slipped and Sir Simon gashed his friend's hand badly. The wound was roughly dressed, but the cut had been deep, and that evening the man came down to dinner with his hands swathed in bandages, complaining that he could not stop the bleeding. Sir Simon, much concerned, took him off to the library. He opened a safe and produced the Penny, which he placed in a basin of water. He then made his friend plunge his hand, bandaged as it was, into the water and keep it there for some time. The bleeding stopped, and next morning the wound was completely healed, except for a small dry scar at the centre.

For generations it is said that a family in Argyll had possession of what was known as *The Red Book of Appin*. Allegedly, within its pages were also magical cures for sick cattle, data on spells to bring on animal fertility, and the secrets of second sight. As recently as the nineteenth century, farmers whose cows became ill or failed to give milk would allegedly go to Appin to consult on their problems. Unfortunately, although the book is associated with the Stewart family, its whereabouts is today unknown. The Lee Penny, however, is in very safe hands.

I contacted Angus Lockhart of the Lee, Chief of the name of Lockhart, to ask if anybody had approached him for assistance during the recent outbreak of foot and mouth disease. Apparently not, although he remembers his father being contacted during a similar plague in the 1960s.

Alas, it would seem that the scientists and politicians who insisted upon mass incineration as the only possible response to such a crisis are as blind to the mysteries of the universe as those worthies of the past who four hundred years ago indicted Isobel Young for witchcraft.

3

Riccio's Grave

So, in the low dens and high-flying garrets of Edinburgh, people may go back upon dark passages in the town's adventures, and chill their marrow with winter's tales about the fire; tales that are singularly apposite and characteristic, not only of the old life, but of the very constitution of built nature in that part, and singularly well qualified to add horror to horror, when the wind pipes around the tall lands, and hoots adown arched passages, and the far-spread wilderness of city lamps keeps quavering and flaring in the gusts.

Robert Louis Stevenson,
Edinburgh: Picturesque Notes

If we have any kind of belief in an afterlife, it makes sense that when traumatic death occurs, earthbound spirits, unprepared for the sudden transition from one state to another, can become trapped in limbo. It similarly follows that such disembodied souls must often have unresolved issues with the past, and this is one explanation for them becoming visible to those who, often as not, have similar sensitivities.

Edinburgh has the reputation of being the most haunted city in Europe. To some extent such myths derive from the Old Town, as it is known, being built on several levels, its shops and residential buildings huddled together on top of a spine of rock that is known as the Royal Mile.

Then again there is the climate, damp and gloomy, with that intense grey mist known locally as the North Sea haar drifting over the city like a shroud from the Firth of Forth, its vapour fingers penetrating deeply into the narrow cobbled streets, closes, wynds and vennels.

Norrie Rowan has been tunnelling under the old town of Edinburgh for over ten years now. Soon after he started it became an obsession, at one stage bankrupting him. Working entirely by hand, he lost three discs from his back in the process and earned himself the title of Edinburgh's Mole Man. 'A lot of love and a lot of pain,' is how he describes it.

It began when he was the owner of the Tron Tavern and began excavation work on his basement. He discovered a passage leading into the first vault under South Bridge and by the time he had finished digging, he had opened up an astonishing network of tunnels under the ground rooms and passages, creating the potential for one long underground street leading from beneath the Royal Mile to Infirmary Street.

A visiting consultant from Disneyland was astonished when shown around it. 'Every city in the USA has a theme park. What you've got here is for real,' he told Norrie. Regardless, the authorities remained unimpressed, offering no financial support, only interference over safety precautions. It was only in 2002, when the *Guinness Book of Records* included the vaults as 'THE most haunted place in Britain,' that people became interested.

However, Norrie is non-committal about the existence of ghosts. He recalls the occasion when a society for the paranormal asked permission to overnight in the diggings behind Merlin's Wynd. 'There were sixteen of them and they were very enthusiastic. They arrived with their sleeping bags and the following morning when I went to let them out, they were all ashen faced. The power card in the electricity meter had run out and they had spent the night in total darkness!'

Now I had also been told of the experiments conducted by Dr Richard Wiseman of the University of Hertfordshire who placed ten volunteers in separate chambers rigged with monitoring equipment. That was a far more organized situation and the subject of a television documentary. Each volunteer individually experienced cold and itching sensations. One heard breathing; another saw a shadowy figure wearing a leather apron.

Of course, there are scientific explanations. The mind plays tricks, but with such a wealth of evidence, it is hard not to believe that something was going on, especially when tests indicated that in the allegedly most haunted rooms there was an increase in air movement. There were also variations in magnetic fields.

Fran Hollinrake, assistant director of Mercat Tours, which organizes walks in the tunnels, has said: 'We may not have proved the existence of ghosts, but we have proved there is something going on down there.'

Lying 40 feet beneath the quadrangle of the City Chambers, is Mary King's Close, a mediaeval street sealed off following an outbreak of plague during the seventeenth century. I consider myself fortunate to have been taken on a tour prior to its commercial redevelopment over the summer of 2002, for whatever the long term consequences of the renovations, it is hard to imagine how it could be made more unsettling than it was before. For a start, most of the passages were bare and starkly lit, and that was what made the ambience so suggestible. Only a few dusty grey areas indicated that dozens of people had once gone about their everyday lives here, but that was enough.

Two friends accompanied me on my tour in January 2002, Sya Simpson, a specialist paint effects expert, and Adrian Shaw, a former television researcher with BBC Scotland. Our guide was David Marriott, telecommunications manager with the City of Edinburgh Council, who had been voluntarily showing visitors around for almost twenty years because, as he confided in us, he truly enjoyed it.

You need somebody like David Marrriott to make such a place come alive, if that is the appropriate response you are looking for.

Once there were approximately one hundred closes and wynds backing off the old High Street, which David likened to 'the spine of a kipper with all the little bones running off on either side.' Alexander King, a man of substantial wealth, was an advocate during the reign of Mary Queen of Scots and bequeathed the properties to his daughter,

Mary, from whom the narrow passage takes its name. From the High Street, it ran downhill on the north side to the shore of the North Loch (today East Princes Street Gardens), which sounds idyllic until you contemplate that the North Loch was nothing much more than the old town sewer. Incredibly, some of the buildings in these constricted streets rose to as many as fourteen and even twenty storeys in height.

It is not surprising, therefore, to discover that post-mediaeval Edinburgh had the reputation of being the 'smelliest, most rat infested place on earth, and a breeding ground for infectious diseases'. In an age of unparalleled medical advance, it is virtually impossible for us to comprehend fully the terror that must have accompanied the outbreak of bubonic plague in 1645, carrying with it a death rate of eighty per cent and more. The only known remedy was evacuation and since the disease had first manifested itself in Mary King's Close, it was decided that the only course of action available was to brick and board up the doors and windows of every dwelling and commercial space from top to bottom.

Not over-wisely, the inhabitants were permitted to leave if they were able, thus carrying the contagion with them, but stories persisted that many had been left behind, folk too ill to move and who were unintentionally sealed up in their homes. What happened to their bones, of course, is anybody's guess.

But thereafter the lodging lay closed for almost one hundred years with one exception. Five years after the plague had subsided, Thomas Coltheard, a wealthy businessman, arrived in the town and began looking for somewhere central for himself and his family to live. He spotted a house in Mary King's Close and despite its reputation, decided that this was just what he had been looking for. His occupancy, however, was to last for only six months.

One night, so the story goes, he was awoken from his sleep by a loud knocking at the front door. When he went to open it, there was nothing outside but a disembodied hand which moved forward to shake his own. The terrified Coltheard retreated back into the hallway, shouting to his wife to fall on her knees and pray.

Undeterred, the hand followed him, and such a din of shouting and screaming ensued that people from the High Street came running down to see what was going on. Witnesses at the time spoke of seeing folk whom they knew to be long dead, with dogs and cats and all manner of livestock scuttling about. It was as if the street had come back to life exactly as it had been before. It was unanimously agreed that this must be the Devil's work and, needless to say, the Coltheard family rapidly sought alternative accommodation.

In the ensuing years, the close began slowly to disappear as the Old Town was re-developed, and by the mid-eighteenth century, following a fire, the merchants of the town decided that the Royal Exchange building, 135 feet from top to bottom, should be erected on the site. This was handed over to the town council in 1811, and since then has served as its headquarters.

Louise Hodgson, who lives in Lanarkshire, is convinced that when she took the tour ten years ago, she saw a small girl crouching in the shadows of a doorway. Her guide told her that others too had described the same figure, a little waif-like infant with a marked face and torn clothes, and this brings me to the most poignant tale associated with Mary King's Close.

Shortly after Louise's visit, David Marriott was asked if he would look after a Japanese medium accompanied by a television film crew. Furthermore, the exercise was to be controlled by members of Edinburgh University's Parapsychology Unit.

David was sceptical. He had done this sort of thing before and not been impressed by the antics of those desperate to record some sort of sensational revelation for their own purposes. Against his finer instincts, however, he reluctantly agreed.

'She arrived and immediately started on about seeing people who were not well,' David recalled. He was not impressed, but then she stopped in the doorway of a small room and announced that she felt a tremendous wave of pain and sadness all around her.

'She stood there for a long time, or at least that is how it seemed,' he said. 'Then she said that she felt something tugging at her trouser leg and looked down to see a small girl with spots on her face. Immediately she started to talk to her in Japanese.'

David thought this absurd because a wee girl in seventeenth-century Edinburgh would never have understood Japanese, but was told that under such circumstances language is not a barrier, communication between alternate worlds is universal.

'The little girl told the medium that she was there because her family had become ill, but she was not on her own. She said that the rooms were full of people. It was a transit area.'

The medium asked her why she was still there, and she replied that she had returned to look for her doll. One of the party was immediately despatched to buy a doll and returned with a tartan figurine, a bit tacky in appearance but probably a wonderment to a child of a bygone age. The Japanese, of course, like their ancestors to be at peace and regularly give them presents. It is part of Japanese culture, but what made a lasting impression on David Marriott is that nobody has spoken of seeing the little girl since.

The story inevitably went the rounds, and on our visit every corner of the small, dusty room, which both Sya and Adrian immediately noted was chillier in temperature than the surrounding passageways, was filled with trinkets: teddy bears, dolls, photographs, ribbons, a tiny purse, mirrors and a bottle of nail varnish.

'When I tell them about it, people always take things out of their pockets and handbags to leave behind,' said David. 'Children are especially touched by her, but I think she must have moved on by now.'

At the foot of the Royal Mile is the Palace of Holyroodhouse, once surrounded on all sides by extensive gardens, woodland and parkland. Old buildings, especially those with a violent past, understandably give rise to ghostly sightings. Perhaps this is because their stories are well documented and our minds better tuned in to the events that once took place there. More recent occurrences tend to go unnoticed, although no doubt, given time, the brand new Scottish Parliament building will produce its fair share of phantoms of the opera.

Alanna Knight, the novelist, believes that the inspiration for one of her most successful books, *The Dagger and the Crown*, began on a childhood excursion to Holyrood. She was sixteen, and for no particular reason other than that she was bored, had wandered away from the main party through a stone-flagged kitchen and an unlocked door to find herself on a narrow path. To her left was a tiny disused burial ground with a padlocked gate. In it were a few small tombstones which looked as if they might have belonged to children or family pets. On her left was the great outer wall of Holyrood Abbey and in front a great fan-spread of lawns, leading into a wide flower border with all kinds of plants, some tall like hollyhocks, right down to pansies. Beyond was a grassy hill empty but for a windmill and a few sheep grazing.

To the right of the path was a mound of freshly dug earth on top of which was a plaque that looked like the top half of the back of a wooden chair. On it was carved in rough letters the name *D. Riccio*.

Alanna went to look for her parents and told them about her discovery, but they were anxious to get home and said they would have a look at it some other time. It was to be thirty years before Alanna returned to the spot and by then everything had changed.

'The first thing that was missing was the old burial ground. The Abbey was there, of course, but the lovely formal garden had gone. There was only a clump of very overgrown rhododendron bushes.'

The greatest shock, however, was that instead of the tree-clad hill with the sheep bleating upon it, she could see the Royal High School on Calton Hill in the distance and the multiple buildings that reach down towards the palace. From what she could remember, these had certainly not been there before, but many of them, she knew, had been firmly established in the landscape for a lot longer than the thirty years since she had last stood in this garden.

This realization, and the puzzle surrounding it, she says, is what first planted the seed for her story based on the plot to kill Lord Darnley, who was implicated in the murder of David Riccio, Mary Queen of Scots's unpopular foreign secretary.

Now we know that Riccio was thrown into the courtyard having been stabbed fifty-seven times, and that Mary, pregnant with Darnley's child, fled from the palace three days later to take refuge first at Dunbar Castle, then in impregnable Edinburgh Castle. But what became of Riccio's body?

It cannot be assumed that he would have been accorded a formal Catholic burial at the time even if the Queen had insisted. In the prevailing religious climate of Protestant Scotland, what actually took place is anybody's guess and most likely the corpse would have been hastily disposed of in an unmarked grave within the palace grounds. Alanna is adamant that what she saw was physically close to the palace itself, and the most probable explanation for this is that her imagination had momentarily tuned into some kind of time warp. She was actually seeing the garden at Holyrood as it had been four hundred years earlier.

On the right hand side of Canongate Kirk, less than half a mile from the palace gates, is a plot marked with a stone upon which the writing is illegible. However, a plaque on the church wall dating from the Victorian era is inscribed: *Tradition says that this is the grave of David Riccio 1533–66 transported from Holyrood.*

But exactly when was the body transported from Holyrood? Immediately after the murder or several years later? Remember that Canongate was an independent burgh until 1639, and Canongate Kirk was not built until 1690. There is no doubt that the grave stone pre-dates this and the Revd Charles Robertson, the present Minister of Canongate Kirk, has no record of what was there before.

Of course, in all probability there were houses, including a property with a garden owned by somebody sympathetic to Mary's unfortunate scribe. It seems most unlikely that the powers that be would have allowed the remains of the passionately High Church Riccio to be interred in a Presbyterian cemetery.

Enter Dr Michael Shea, former press secretary to the Queen, and today chairman of the Independent Broadcasting Authority in Scotland. 'At Holyrood there are marks on the turf at the back of the palace that have been there for centuries,' he said. Old maps indeed disclose that there was a network of walled gardens within the immediate-policies, and especially after continuous rain or sustained heat, their shapes can sometimes be made out beneath the grass.

'There is no *here* and *there*, only *here*,' says the Revd Charles Robertson. 'There is no *now* and *then*, only *now*. Time and place belong to the eternal here and now, and we dip in and out of them constantly.'

Robertson maintains that in his opinion, those who have gone before are always with us here and now. That, he believes, is the basis of the Communion of the Saints. 'The Holy Trinity is a way of explaining why we relate to the past as if it is the present. If we live in God, Father, Son and Holy Spirit, and God is in every place, every time, then we too are with him in every place and time. Eternity is all part and parcel of the same breath that I am drawing now.'

Although he has no personal experience to substantiate it, he is aware that his predecessor, the Revd Dr Ronald Selby Wright, was convinced that Canongate Kirk, the manse, and adjacent Acheson House all had non-visible residents. 'There is a double strand of evidence of people coming into the kirk and subconsciously finding themselves in a room full of nineteenth-century tables and chairs and lamps, and seeing figures moving about,' he said. 'Ronnie often told me that he had come face to face with somebody who wasn't there, but who had always been there. The experience, he said, was half-conscious and momentary, and it repeated itself on further occasions.'

Slippages of time and place are commonplace phenomena, and for many go unnoticed. Others, however, are more receptive despite their finer instincts.

In fashionable India Street, *Scottish Daily Mail* columnist Colette Douglas-Home has sometimes felt that she was not alone in her kitchen. 'The sensation is that someone is standing behind me,' she said. 'Then when you turn around there is nobody there.' In the same street, the late society photographer Brodrick Haldane frequently saw a shadowy figure in his hallway. 'Off the ground,' recalls his friend Michael Thornton, who shared the experience when staying for a weekend. 'I was on the telephone in the kitchen and somebody flashed past the door. Only there was no upper half, just legs. The building dates from 1819, and we later discovered that the floor levels had been altered during the late-Victorian era.'

In Royal Terrace, Carol Hogel and her daughter have on different occasions both woken during the night to see an exceptionally plain girl in the room wearing a beautiful, high-necked dress embroidered with tiny roses. It was the tiny roses that convinced them that this was not just a dream. 'When we compared notes we realized that we had both noticed the dress. The impression I got was that she must be a spinster daughter possibly staying at home to look after an elderly parent She looked so sad and so terribly lonely,' reflected Carol afterwards.

4

The Secrets of Rosslyn

Blazed battlement and pinnet high,
Blazed every rose-carved buttress fair —
So still they blaze, when fate is nigh
The Lordly line of high St Clair.

Sir Walter Scott,
The Lay of the Last Minstrel

For some it is simply a gem of Gothic architectural genius tucked away at one end of a wooded, river gorge immediately south of Edinburgh. For others, it is a spiritual time capsule; a Dr Who's Tardis standing ready to transport true believers into another dimension.

For generations, the tiny fifteenth century Rosslyn Chapel has both confounded and intrigued historians, inspiring others to believe that the extraordinarily complex carvings within its portals are coded messages from the past holding the secrets to the meaning of life itself.

The result is that rumours proliferate.

There is talk of hidden treasure, not just any old treasure, but untold riches, religious artefacts and scrolls from the original Temple of Jerusalem, even the Holy Grail itself. Another, and for many blasphemous, suggestion is that the celebrated Apprentice Pillar was created to conceal the skull of Jesus Christ himself.

Absurd, ridiculous, even after centuries of speculation nobody is any the wiser. Since the chapel is privately owned, permission from the Rosslyn Chapel Trust to excavate has not been forthcoming. Furthermore, the ground underneath has been designated an historic site by Historic Scotland, and since graves are involved, the legal Right of Sepulchre would have to be overcome.

Yet those in favour of further investigation remain adamant. For the carvings and decorations to be found within Rosslyn Chapel are no ordinary religious motifs. They represent almost every spiritual influence which existed in the centuries before the chapel was built: Greek, Babylonian, Egyptian, Hebrew, and pagan Norse. For instance, there are over one hundred carvings of the Green Man, the most potent Celtic symbol of fertility and re-birth.

But even to begin to understand what this is all about, you have to search back over seven hundred years, starting with the St Clair family of neighbouring Roslin Castle, and their association with the heretical order of the Knights Templar, for two hundred years the most powerful religious and military force that Europe has ever known.

Founded in 1119 by a Burgundian knight named Hugo de Payns, whose wife was Catherine de St Clair of Roslin, and Godeffroi de St Omer, a knight from northern France, the order's pious origins lay in protecting the pilgrims who, after the first crusade, flocked to Jerusalem and other sacred spots of the Holy Land.

In recognition of their services, Baldwin I, King of Jerusalem, soon after made over to them part of his royal palace next to the former mosque of al-Aksa, the so-called 'Temple of Solomon', from which they took their name. Although essentially military in concept, the knights rapidly established themselves as a religious community, living in chastity, obedience and poverty, according to the rule of St Benedict, to 'fight with a pure mind for the supreme and true king'.

And such was their success in the subsequent crusades, that by the mid-thirteenth century it looked as if their power knew no boundaries. Their property, with castles and manors estimated at between

7,050 and 9,000, was scattered throughout every country in Christendom, from Denmark to Spain, from Ireland to Cyprus.

Spiritual privileges were granted to them by popes as lavishly as temporal possessions were by princes and people. Pope Adrian IV allowed them to have their own churches. Eugenius III exempted their churchyards from ordinary excommunications and interdicts, which meant that those who died outside of the Holy Roman church often found a last resting place in the consecrated grounds of the Templars.

But the fabled wealth of the Templars came not so much from their territorial possessions and the legacies which they accumulated, but from their being great international bankers and financiers. In the twelfth and thirteenth centuries, the Paris Temple became the centre of the world's money market. Popes and kings deposited their revenues, and these vast sums were not hoarded but issued as loans on adequate security.

For two hundred years the Knights Templar were an indomitable force, but the end, when it came, was both swift and ruthless. Never had they appeared stronger than immediately before their ruin, but it was exactly because of this that their downfall became inevitable.

They had simply become too powerful, inciting the jealousy of the very people, kings and Pope, who had made their creation possible. Even the rituals of their society, designed to protect them, were turned against them with charges of pagan idolatry and sodomy. The laws that governed the Templars' conduct, such as travelling in pairs and not attacking unless provoked three times, were interpreted as base immorality.

Persecuted on every front, their leaders arrested in 1307, the Knights Templar who survived did so by taking refuge in Portugal and Scotland where, having played a major role in supporting the Scots against the English, they went underground to create what in the centuries since has emerged as Freemasonry. The whereabouts of their great treasure, rumoured to have been spirited away to safety as their enemies closed in, has baffled historians ever since.

So why did the Templars flee to Scotland? There are two obvious reasons. First, that the Scots King Robert the Bruce, had the year before himself been excommunicated by the Pope for his involvement with the murder of his cousin, the Red Comyn, in Dumfries. Secondly, Scotland was the home base of the St Clairs of Roslin.

Bruce wanted the expertise of these

fighting knights, something which in 1314 he skilfully put to use in achieving his great victory against the English at Bannockburn. It is estimated that 432 Templar Knights, including Sir Henry St Clair, Baron of Roslin, and his sons William and Henry, took part in the historic charge which won the day.

Warned thereafter by Bruce to keep a low profile, the persecuted knights' response was to re-invent themselves as Freemasons. Once established, the Hereditary Grand Mastership of the Masonic Guilds was to remain with the St Clair family until St Andrew's Day in 1736 when yet another Sir William of Roslin resigned his hereditary patronage and protectorships of the Masonic Craft in order to inaugurate the Grand Lodge of Ancient, Free and Accepted Masons of Scotland.

The first Roslin Castle was built on the site of the present chapel on College Hill in the eleventh century. Walderne de Saint Claro, had accompanied William the Conqueror from Normandy on his 1066 invasion of England, and his son by Margaret, daughter of Richard of Normandy, was one of the many Anglo-Norman barons who came north to settle in Scotland during the reign of David I and was granted the barony of Roslin. This was confirmed to his son, Sir William St Clair, and thereafter the family played a crucial role in virtually every stage of Scotland's turbulent history.

The story goes that Sir William, returning from the Battle of Roslin Moor in 1302, had taken an English prisoner of some distinction. In return for his being well entertained by his captor, the Englishman recommended that Sir William relocate his castle on the nearby promontory surrounded on three sides by the River Esk.

Sir William took his advice, but it was not until two centuries later that the chapel was erected upon the site once occupied by the first castle. In the meantime, the St Clair family had prospered.

Almost immediately following the suppression of the Knights Templar in Europe, it was noted that the fortunes of the St Clairs had improved dramatically. In his 1835 *Geneaologie of the Saint Claires of Rosslyn*, Father R. A. Hay writes that Lords of St Clair were everywhere escorted by four hundred mounted knights, and their ladies were attended by eighty ladies-in-waiting. Furthermore, towards the end of the century, through marriage, they inherited the earldom of Orkney.

Henry St Clair, Earl of Orkney, therefore became a prince, and having discovered Greenland, embarked upon a voyage to the

Americas, landing in Nova Scotia and travelling as far south as Maine. This was a good one hundred years before Christopher Columbus was credited with the discovery of the New World.

With his Scots and Norse connections, and talk of a Northern Commonwealth of Scandinavia, Scotland, Ireland, and lands across the seas, this extraordinary man proved too much for the English and they had him murdered on his return.

Rosslyn Chapel was built by his grandson, the third and last St Clair Earl of Orkney, who also held the curious title of 'Knight of the Cockle and Golden Fleece'. A patron of crafts masonry throughout Europe, he had both the contacts and means at his disposal to create something extraordinary, and this he most certainly set out to do.

Since Scotland was the resting place chosen by the Templars for their treasures and secrets, it could be concluded that Rosslyn Chapel was erected especially as a memorial to their existence. As it transpired, however, Earl William's death in 1484 meant that the large collegiate church which he had intended to build was never completed, which is probably just as well. It is hard to imagine how the inevitable splendour of such a place of worship could possibly have survived the religious upheavals which were to take place in Scotland a century later.

In fact, only the choir was finished, and this, standing on thirteen pillars which create an arcade of twelve pointed arches, is dazzling enough. A fourteenth pillar between the two at the east end, forms the division between the nave and the Lady Chapel. The roof is barrel-vaulted in stone and dotted with images of stars, lilies and roses. There are carvings of the constellation of the Zodiac, dragons, the orb of the sun, the engrailed cross and images of American corn and cacti, again created forty odd years before Columbus landed on that continent, and it is such carvings that hold the attention, amazing visitors throughout the centuries.

But other aspects of Rosslyn Chapel are equally thought provoking. When Sir Walter Scott published *The Lay of the Last Minstrel* in 1805, he wrote of twenty of Roslin's barons bold buried in the vaults.

Seem'd all on fire that chapel proud,
    Where Roslin's chiefs uncoffin'd lie;
Each Baron, for a sable shroud,
    Sheathed in his iron panoply.

Up until the seventeenth century, all but one of the male members of the St Clair family are said to have been interred coffinless, but wearing their knightly armour. The assumption is that within the airless vaults, the bodies are perfectly preserved and ready to rise again at the Resurrection.

Seismic studies conducted by Edinburgh University in the 1980s certainly revealed that there are metallic objects within the vaults, but there is also the possibility of discovering ancient scrolls and the Holy Rood itself, not to mention Royal jewels sent to the St Clairs for safe keeping at the time of Henry VIII's Rough Wooing.

Again, nobody knows for sure.

Then we have also the tale of the Apprentice Pillar to take into account, with the completed article as evidence.

The story goes that a master mason, having received instructions from his patron as to the required design, was hesitant to carry out the work until he had been to Rome for inspiration. He consequently went abroad and while he was away an apprentice, having dreamed what the finished pillar would look like, set about the work. When the master mason returned he was so outraged at the beauty of what his apprentice had done that he killed him in a fit of rage and jealousy. It is said that he was hanged for the deed.

Apocryphal or not, the carved heads of

both the murdered apprentice and his executioner can be seen to this day amid the puzzle of symbols and mediaeval graffiti that continues to intrigue us.

For over five hundred years, Rosslyn Chapel has kept its secrets, yet almost weekly there are approaches from some academic body or another to undertake further ground scans of the vaults and to examine the walls of the building. There is even talk of excavating the vaults.

Will then the wisdom of Solomon finally be revealed to us through the mystical legacy of the Knights Templar? Is this a time machine programmed to take us to the stars and will our destiny be cast up before us as in some Indiana Jones fantasy? Or is it just some monumental mediaeval joke?

Some would say that in the way of fate, such things are best left alone.

5

The Silverbuthall Ghost

I didn't want to happen to me
What happened to Thomas the Rhymer —
Especially as he awoke
With a tongue
That could never lie.

Norman McCaig,
'Walking Home Exhausted'

As every true Borderer knows, King Arthur sleeps under the Eildons. Because of this, true Border folk are universally open to flights of fancy. The landscape that surrounds them not only lies at the heart of this, it inspires and encourages them.

For a period during the 1980s, I enjoyed the tenancy of Hopecarton, a shepherd's cottage on Drumelzier farm, near Broughton, in Peeblesshire. Long and idyllic summer days were passed walking on those tree-less, lonely hills between Tweedsmuir, Talla and the Meggat Valley which was flooded to create a second great reservoir serving the taps of Edinburgh far away to the north.

Naturally I was aware of the prophecy of Thomas the Rhymer: 'When Tweed and Powsayle meet at Merlin's grave, Scotland and England that day ae king shall have.' As foretold, that burial spot, which tradition has beneath a thorn tree on the river's edge at Drumelzier, did flood approximately four hundred years after the prophecy was made. The date was 25 July 1603, and on that day James VI of Scotland was crowned James I of England, thus unifying two nations who have never quite forgiven him for doing so.

By pinpointing Merlin's grave, True Thomas, as he became known, was endorsing the Scottish version of the Arthurian legend where the hero is a prince of Strathclyde in the sixth century. Fleeing from a great battle in the ancient Forest of Caledon, Arthur's sage, the druidic Merlin, was allegedly stoned to death by shepherds in the service of Meldredus, a local warlord, who left him to die on the banks of the Tweed.

It is hard to dismiss the imagery surrounding the mythology, which if anything can only be upstaged by the allegories of Thomas's own seven-year abduction by the Queen of the faeries. In the Scottish Borderland, the points of reference are everywhere. In his book *Arthur and the Lost Kingdoms*, Alistair

Moffat, former managing director of Scottish Television Enterprises, points to the surviving place names associated with Thomas's kidnapping — the Eildon Tree, Boglie Burn and Huntly Bank — as confirmation of this visit to the Celtic Otherworld, a thought much to be contemplated on 31 October, Samhuinn Eve, when the barriers between the worlds of man and the supernatural are lowered.

To a far greater extent than Hugo de Gifford, and their near contemporary the necromancer Michael Scott, it is True Thomas who sets the scene for all subsequent Borders folklore. Looming large over all of them is the giant shadow of Sir Walter Scott. And although Sir Walter was, to begin with, the all time sceptic on the subject of the occult, towards the end of his life he had become fixated with it to the extent that in his latter journals he records an encounter with his dead wife.

The A701 runs south from Broughton, alongside the Devil's Beef Tub, a vast hollow in the hills where Border reivers hid their stolen cattle. For some years Debbie Masraff and her husband owned and managed the Crook Inn here, a former posting house visited by Robert Burns who stopped and penned a poem in the bar. The Crook Inn dates from 1604, and although the entire area is steeped in fable, Debbie says that she never saw the resident ghost that the previous owners had talked about. What she did see, on several occasions, was a small West Highland terrier which followed her from room to room.

What made this all the more bizarre was that the Masraffs kept Jack Russells which under normal circumstances would most certainly have seen off any newcomer without hesitation. In this instance, they did not seem to mind. 'At first I thought it must have belonged to one of our guests, but then I would have known about it,' she said. 'And it didn't belong to anybody local so far as I know.'

Otherwise, it did not bother her too much, apart from her not knowing who its owner was. The Westie became a regular at the Crook Inn right up until the Masraffs sold up and moved on. 'It would just suddenly be there, just behind me, and then it would vanish,' said Debbie. 'I grew rather fond of it.'

West of Melrose stands Darnick Tower, one of the best surviving examples of a Borders keep, built to protect the surrounding countryside from the marauding bands of English raiders who came in waves throughout the thirteenth, fourteenth and fifteenth centuries. Theresa Wilson has lived at

Darnick Tower for over forty years and although well aware that the walls have stories to tell, has never at any time felt uncomfortable there. Nevertheless, when son Felix Sear, who today runs the Wynd Theatre in Melrose, brought her 2½ year old grand-daughter Harriet to stay with her, Theresa was reluctant to allow the little girl to wander around unaccompanied. For generations there had been stories of a ghostly monk from Melrose Abbey being seen at Darnick, and one room in particular was associated with him.

Of course, the inevitable happened. Harriet was tucked up in bed, but somehow managed to climb out and find her way from the bedroom, through the drawing room and up the steep tower staircase without being noticed. An hour had passed before her parents and Theresa discovered her missing, only to find her coming down the stairs smiling and laughing. When they asked her what she had been doing, she said, 'Talking to such a nice old man.'

'What did he look like?' asked her father.

'He had a sort of duffle coat on,' she replied.

When the family went to inspect the room, it was empty.

Although in this case we may never know

who the 'nice old man' was, there is at least some evidence as to his calling and where he came from. In other instances, a certain amount of detective work becomes necessary if we want to try and establish who somebody is, or might have been.

A group of twelve-year-olds at Hawick High School were recently invited to write a short essay on their town, and as was to be expected, the majority had comments to make on the knitwear factories, the Common Riding, the youth and leisure centres, and the local monuments. The essays are full of character and observation, but what is fascinating is the number of references to the Silverbuthall ghost.

According to Craig and Teresa, everybody in Hawick knows about it. Danielle thought that it was a lady ghost, and Laura wrote that it was because of the stories she had heard about the ghost that she liked living in Hawick. Kevin, who had actually lived for a time in Silverbuthall Road, insisted that there had been strange goings on in the street for at least four to five years. 'One time my Mum was reading a book and the TV came on all by itself, and when my Mum put it off, it came on again. Another time I broke one of my Mum's ornaments and my Dad said he'd fix it in the morning. In the morning it was fixed, but none of us had touched it.' On that basis, Kevin didn't think it was a bad ghost.

Researching into the past of the Silver-buthall estate it emerges that during the first half of the nineteenth century it was owned by the Scott family. Prior to its demolition in 1921, a fine Victorian mansion house had been erected and was lived in by a James Laidlaw, described as 'a manufacturer'.

The Laidlaws also owned Hazlewood House, which stood some 300 yards from Silverbuthall, and there are two sources of origin given to the name. The first, that it was the site of an archery competition for a silver arrow. The second, rather more apocryphal, is that when the architect suggested he build two more turrets on to what had by then begun to look like a mansion in a Walt Disney film, James Laidlaw replied, 'Aye, but it'd cost a lot more siller bits.'

It did, and eventually the siller bits' must have run out, for during the 1920s, Silverbuthall was put up for sale. Surprisingly, for such a fine looking mansion, there were no takers, and the fabric of the building steadily fell into disrepair until it was eventually acquired by the town council.

By the 1940s the grounds of Silverbuthall were over-run with rows of prefab housing, part of a national re-habilitation programme, in other words slum clearance. The prefabs were intended as a temporary measure, but remained for over twenty years until the present Silverbuthall housing estate was developed in 1961.

So who exactly is or was the ghost of Silverbuthall? A former resident of the big house, perhaps? Or was he or she a runaway from the prefabs? Time moves on. Old memories fade and dim. Nobody can be certain. However, Colin Moxey, who lives on Silverbuthall Road, recently had his photograph taken by his daughter in the garden. When the picture was developed, standing behind him, looking over the fence, is a pale face with what looks like a Victorian-style moustache. 'It was a Polaroid photo, so the negative couldn't have been tampered with,' he says.

Colin Moxey has always had odd feelings in that particular area of his garden, to the left of the greenhouse. When he first built the garden shed, it somehow managed to move 2 feet all by itself during the night. 'I'd recently dug up the ground before erecting the shed, and I think it may have had something to do with that,' he says.

Another Hawick haunting concerns the murder of Sir George Fernielaw in the early fifteenth century by the Laird of Langlands.

Allegedly there was a dispute over money, and Sir George, who had become a monk, was summoned to a meeting with his landlord. They came to blows, and Sir George's head was cut off with the laird's sword. Taken for trial before King James IV in Edinburgh, Langlands managed to persuade the king that he was innocent because he had only struck off the monk's cowl. What he failed to explain, and what seemingly nobody pointed out, was that the monk's head had been in it.

For four years Ernie Corson lived at Fernielaw Place, close to where a cross was erected in Sir George's memory. Having a weak bladder, he would get out of bed to go to the bathroom every night, and every time there would be a figure moving on the stair landing, gliding very fast. 'It looked like a woman wearing a dress with a hood,' he said. 'It was three-dimensional. My first thought was that somebody had broken into the house, but there was nobody there. And then I saw it again the following night, and the next. I didn't like to tell anyone about it as I thought they'd think I'd had a turn, but then one day my son began saying that there was something funny about the house when he came home late at night. Two weeks before we moved out, I saw the figure again, this time downstairs. It just stood there in the centre of the room with its arms folded, wearing a greyish-brown garment. Then it was gone.'

After this, Ernie and his wife moved to live in a flat at Wilton Lodge Museum, which had been the historic home of the Langlands family. While looking through some old papers, he came across the story of the murder and realized at once that it must have been the monk he had seen. 'Fernielaw Place is on the spot where Sir George lived,' he explained.

The sleepy hollow of Lilliesleaf on the Ale Water, south-east of Selkirk, is home to the Hedges family, who six years ago moved into one of a row of cottages on the main street, at one time occupied by the families of local agricultural workers. In such rural surroundings, it is an idyllic lifestyle, with the children attending schools locally, and Lorraine working in the village as a computer programmer.

To begin with, however, it was Katherine Hedges, Lorraine's eldest daughter, who became aware that they were not alone in the cottage. It was her birthday, and she had been given a new bubble bath and a body spray. A couple of friends had come over and afterwards, when she went upstairs to her room, there was a strong smell of scent. Immediately she saw that the can of body spray was empty and that the bubble bath was spread over the sheets of the bed and the fireplace.

Nobody had been in her room. Her brother Andrew was out, and her mother was playing with Rebecca downstairs. Besides, Rebecca was then too small to reach up to the fireplace. It was a complete mystery, but not for long.

One evening she was sitting in her room with her friend Kerrie and all of a sudden both of them saw the brown outline of a man against a wall. 'He was wearing a pointed hat and had a large nose,' she says. Thereafter she often felt his presence and saw a black, blurry outline that came and went. When she told her mother about it, Lorraine to begin with thought that it was just teenage imagination. And then she began to see things too.

'Kathy was telling me all of these things and I was very tied up doing a degree in computing at the time. Then it started. On one occasion, a little boy came running down the stairs and smiled at me as he ran past.'

Lorraine would wake up during the night to find people in her room, a woman with a child to begin with. 'They came towards me and then seemed to pass over me and through the wall,' she says. 'I thought I must be hallucinating, so I tried to come to terms with it by putting it out of my head. Then it happened again. The room always became incredibly still and very cold. They were there again, but they didn't seem to be unpleasant or threatening.'

Eventually, however, she had a horrid experience. The children were away with their father for the weekend. Lorraine was in the house on her own, and awoke in the small hours to find a large, solid figure watching over her.

'He was a round, unshaven man with a very ugly rough face,' she recalls. 'Something made me think he must have been in the navy, although I can't think why. Anyway, I had one of those big American torches beside the bed and reached over for it, but then I discovered that I couldn't get to it. I was frozen rigid with terror, and then, like the others, he moved towards me very slowly and passed over my head through the wall.'

Shaken, Lorraine telephoned her friend Fred, who also lives in the village. He immediately told her to pack her things and to come over for the night. The next day he and Lynn Williams, another neighbour, accompanied Lorraine back to the cottage to investigate, Fred informing them that the centre of the village was positioned on top of an historic ley line. Some people believe ley lines to be mystical linkages between prehistoric sites. Others are convinced that they follow routes of cosmic energy within the earth. In other words, they form a pathway between unknown dimensions.

Once they had looked around, Lynn, who had never been inside the house before, drew out a plan of the rooms on a sheet of paper and without being told, instantly identified where Lorraine and Katherine had seen their visitors. At this point Lorraine became extremely anxious, and paid a visit to the local minister, the Revd Frank Campbell. He was very sympathetic and arranged to visit the cottage with a couple of colleagues. They said a few prayers, and since that day there have been no further incidents.

However, just to make sure, Lorraine moved all the furniture in the rooms around and placed a big sunny picture over the wall that had been behind her bed. 'But it was a long time before I could go to sleep without the light on,' she says.

6

Flying Sources

How often have I said to you that when you have eliminated the impossible, whatever remains, however improbable, must be the truth.

Sir Arthur Conan Doyle,
Sherlock Holmes: The Sign of Four

Poltergeists are the most common form of domestic manifestation, notable for throwing things about, plucking the bedclothes from mortals as they sleep, and making unexpected and inexplicable noises, day and night. Such phenomena are most frequently associated with one person, often a child, possibly suffering from sexual frustration, a nervous malady or recent nervous shock.

Long ago, for instance, there was a classic case centred on the daughter of a Captain Molesworth, a resident of Trinity, in Edinburgh, whose daughter began suffering from a deep depression following the death of her sister. All kinds of curious sounds and unexplained breakages started to infest the semi-detached villa in which they lived, and the captain, refusing to believe that these could originate from his own home, bored holes into the wall of the attached house convinced that his neighbour was making fun of him.

Now it just so happened that it was his landlord who occupied the adjoining house, and this gentleman was sufficiently unimpressed by the damage to his property that he brought a suit against the captain in the sheriff's court. Alas, the outcome was insubstantial, but what was suggested during the proceedings, although nobody was inclined to pursue such accusations, is that Miss Molesworth's unhappy moods were closely implicated with the aberrations that had taken place.

In Cockburn Street, which drops steeply down from the Old Town of Edinburgh's High Street, there is a café called the Toddle Inn, and when Lola, the manageress, opens the doors in the morning, she has become used to finding that objects have been moved about overnight. 'But there is nothing unpleasant or threatening about it,' she insists.

However, two years ago a group of workmen involved in repairing the tunnels

64

under the street had a very different reaction. 'They wouldn't say what it was all about,' says Lola. 'Only that they were terrified, and none of them could be persuaded to go back down there again. And big strapping lads they were too.'

What is also worth bearing in mind is that poltergeist activity, although certainly prevalent in days gone by, is very much a modern, contemporary manifestation. Again, many of those who have experienced it are not prepared to talk about it. In some reported cases, the activity has become so frenetic that those associated with it have felt they had no alternative but to move away from where it was taking place. Even then, it has been known to follow them, but then there are others who find themselves in the same situation and are entirely unaffected by it.

For the three years before she married, Janet Wotherspoon shared a flat with three girlfriends in Marchmont, on Edinburgh's Southside. They were all teenagers at the time and enjoying the lives that freedom away from home, school and parental supervision brings with it — parties, boys, and alcohol.

'They were fun, carefree days,' says Janet.

But then all sorts of odd mishaps began to take place.

'Perhaps it was to do with raging

hormones, but I do find that hard to believe,' she reflects. 'The trouble was that because I was the one who was always there over the three years, while the other girls came and went, I was the one who got blamed. I suppose officially I was the landlady, although I did not really think of myself as such. When odd things happened, the others all thought I was playing tricks on them.'

In general the occurrences were inconsequential, but over a period of time they began to unsettle all of the girls. Mostly they involved electrical appliances. The cooker rings would be turned on when one or other of them went into the kitchen, and Radio Four, which teenage girls never listen to, would be playing. They began to accuse one another of negligence, but nobody would admit to having used the cooker or listening to the radio. Then a kettle would boil without anyone having switched it on, and hairdryers would suddenly start blowing hot air.

'It all became a bit mad,' says Janet. 'We would wake up in the morning and there would be a jug of water on the bedside. We'd probably drunk quite a bit the night before, but nobody remembered taking a jug of water to bed with them. A glass, maybe. But not a jug!'

Then one night one of the girls, left alone

in the flat over the weekend, heard a crawling noise coming from the kitchen. She was absolutely terrified, and when she heard the milkman making his delivery in the early hours she flung open the door and begged him to come in and investigate. He must have thought Christmas had come early, but when there was no sign of disturbance human or otherwise in the kitchen, he was promptly dismissed. On another occasion, one of Janet's oldest friends came to stay for three weeks and moved out after two nights. 'There is definitely something very weird about this place,' she told Janet.

Janet's ultimate confrontation involved a copy of the *Edinburgh Evening News*. She had bought it to find out what was on at the cinema, but when she turned to pick it up from the table where she thought she had left it, it was no longer there. She went into the hall to see if she had left it there, but she hadn't, and when she came back into the sitting room there it was on the table. She quickly looked up the information she had wanted and threw the newspaper into the rubbish bin. An hour later it was back on the table once more. She concluded that one of her flatmates must have rescued it to read, and threw it away again. Later on, it was back on the table.

'That was when I flipped,' she says. 'I picked up a knife and stabbed it before I threw it away this time. Stabbing it obviously did the trick because this time it did not reappear.'

For Neil and Mary Blackburn, who own Fernie Castle Hotel at Letham in Fife, objects being moved around are part of daily life and, according to a medium who recently visited them, the spirits of children are responsible. The Blackburns have owned Fernie Castle for four years and during the restoration work all kinds of inexplicable goings-on took place.

For example, Neil was on top of a ladder in the midst of decorating the drawing room when the paintbrush he was using fell to the floor. In the meantime, a member of staff came into the room and placed some keys on the mantelpiece. Neil carried on working with another brush and then turned to find that the first brush had been placed on the mantelpiece while the bunch of keys had somehow attached itself to his tool belt.

The Blackburns have no explanation for the young couple with a baby who stayed overnight and left early in the morning complaining of a shaking bed. 'It's not a frequent occurrence,' says Neil.

Then again, there was the guest who

retired to her bedroom in the west tower after a superb dinner and who was just about to fall asleep when there was a knock at the door. When she went to open it, there was nobody there. It happened again, so she decided to sleep with the light on.

The following night, the same occurrence took place, but this time, in the middle of the night, a lady appeared wearing a green dress and then disappeared. Neil Blackburn confirms that this was probably the Green Lady, who has been known to appear from time to time in the west tower.

Fernie Castle was built by the Fairlie Family, then passed to the Balfours. The story goes that in the nineteenth century a young runaway couple turned up to stay at the castle, hotly pursued by the lady's irate father. They had hidden in the tiny room at the top of the west tower and were found there by her father's men. In the struggle to escape, she tripped and fell three floors to her death. It is she who is said to be the Green Lady, although to date nobody has been able to identify her name.

In the meantime, Neil Blackburn is pretty relaxed about his houseguests, paying and otherwise. 'The children don't mean any harm, nor does the Green Lady,' he says. 'There has been the odd occasion when a glass has been inexplicably broken, but generally speaking we feel that it adds something to the interest of the old place.'

Sometimes, of course, no-nonsense poltergeists can prove themselves to be an unexpected bonus. Angus and Sara Munzie, with their children Pete and Janine, moved into their new home in Cumbernauld when Angus was headhunted to work for a packaging and marketing company located nearby. They were delighted with the house which was furnished with every modern requirement, including a dishwasher and satellite television. To begin with all was well. The kids settled into their new school without incident and received favourable reports when one or other of their parents attended the regular parent/teacher meetings. Unfortunately, the nature of Angus's job meant that he was often away on business and Sara, who found a job with flexible hours in a local roadhouse, had to shoulder much of the burden of parenthood at a time when Pete was becoming increasingly obsessed with football, and Janine, with boys.

Nobody remembers quite when the anomalies started — items of shopping went missing, ornaments were mysteriously broken and the cat's litter tray moved from room to room — but the first major incident took place in November 2001. Sara had just arrived home in the family's Ford Mondeo when she saw flames inside the kitchen window. Rushing indoors, she discovered that the refuse bin was on fire and, quick witted, poured the contents of the kettle over it. Thankfully, there was little or no damage.

Apart from Janine, who was upstairs in her bedroom and insisted that she had been nowhere near the kitchen, there was nobody in the house. Two days later Sara returned from her workplace to discover that the entire sitting room had been moved about, furniture placed in different positions and pictures re-hung on the walls. Once again, only Janine was at home and denied any knowledge of it.

At the time Janine was aged sixteen and when not in her bedroom, on-line with her computer, would sometimes in the evenings meet up with her friends in the town centre or take the bus into Glasgow. Where her mother was concerned, what they got up to was anybody's guess. Increasingly there were arguments about homework and the tidiness of her room, and eventually Sara, a normally relaxed and calm person, lost her temper and uncharacteristically shouted at Janine that if she did not tidy her room, she was not to go out. Janine responded by picking up all of the clothes, magazines and make-up she had scattered over the floor and on her bed, and she threw everything into the large fitted wardrobe on the right hand side of the room. She then took off. When she returned home around 9 p.m., she found that her bedroom door was blocked. There was no lock, but something seemed to be wedged across it.

Fortunately Angus was back from a sales trip abroad, and with Pete's help succeeded in forcing the door open with brute strength. Once inside, however, they were baffled. The fitted wardrobe had somehow managed to detach itself from the wall onto which it was held in place by six screws, and had fallen over sideways to block the doorway. Nobody from outside could have done this. The bedroom windows were double glazed and closed, and there were no other means of getting into the room.

What made the entire saga even more baffling was that, apart from the magazines, the wardrobe was empty and Janine's clothes had gone. Their first thought was that they must have been stolen, but shortly afterwards, when Sara glanced out of the window they were lying scattered about on the flagstone pathway below. This was doubly peculiar owing to the windows being firmly shut.

'No, I wasn't responsible,' said Sara indignantly. 'We asked our priest over to talk about it and told him about the fire and the furniture moving about. He spent a long time going from room to room on his own and then called up somebody on the phone to come and join him. They did the same thing all over again, going in and out of the rooms and sprinkling holy water. Since then there's been nothing odd to report. I'm just glad it's over. The one good thing that came out of it is that Janine now either puts everything away in drawers or hangs them up. She even pulls up her duvet cover when she gets out of bed in the morning. Her room has never looked so immaculate.'

7

The Red Room at Borthwick

This seemed to be a supernatural suggestion that piety alone could relieve me from the evil spirit. I was much impressed with it, and my devotion was fervent today.

James Boswell

Borthwick Castle is a formidable looking edifice with twin towers rising darkly against the bland Midlothian landscape. A few miles from the small hamlet of Gorebridge, off the A7, it was erected in the fifteenth century and gained its main notoriety when Mary Queen of Scots took refuge there for three weeks in 1567 following her ill-fated elopement with the Earl of Bothwell.

Although five centuries on it is still owned by the Borthwick family, it is today leased out as a hotel and rightly capitalizes on its dramatic past. With its great stone hallway, towering ceilings, and 14-feet thick walls, the interiors are the very stuff of which ghostly fantasies are made. Hitherto, they have never failed to disappoint.

In 1979, Scottish Television sent reporter Nicholas Radcliffe and a camera team to investigate reports of strange goings-on in the Red Room. Nicholas Radcliffe is a balanced individual who claims to be the all-time cynic when it comes to the paranormal, yet freely admits that he has absolutely no explanation for what took place that night.

'We set up our lights and camera in the Red Room, and after dinner rather childishly started to play around with a ouija board,' he recalls. 'We were pretty light-hearted and had been larking about when suddenly the movements became very erratic and the board spelled out that the cameraman was unwelcome and that if the producer and I were to stay, we must remove all of the recording equipment from the room instantly. We didn't take this particularly seriously, but all the same did as we were asked. In the meantime, the cameraman said he was off to join his wife who had been feeling unwell and was in the bedroom upstairs.'

Nicholas and his producer then went for a nightcap in the Great Hall, but in the middle of a second dram of Talisker were interrupted by an extraordinary noise. 'The only way I can possibly describe it is to say that it sounded like a stampede of pigs, a high-pitched squealing and shrieking coming from the staircase,' he says. 'When I opened the door to see what on earth was going on, the sound faded, but there was our cameraman lying unconscious on the bottom step with a gash on his forehead and blood all over his shirt.'

An ambulance was called which took an age to arrive. However, when it did, the cameraman was seen to by two paramedics, his cut bandaged up, and he was taken up to the bedroom where his wife was already in a deep sleep. Nicholas and the producer spent the night in the Red Room with no untoward disturbances or manifestations taking place, then assembled at breakfast the following morning to find the cameraman and his wife looking well-rested and in good humour.

Nicholas admits that he was frankly astonished. 'I asked him how he was feeling and what had happened to his cut, and he said he had no idea what I was talking about. He insisted that he had gone straight to bed after leaving us in the Red Room, and that he had slept like a baby. His wife confirmed this. Also, he was wearing the same shirt and there was not a spot of blood to be seen on it anywhere.'

So what about his falling down the stairs

and the bandage and the ambulance being called out?

'There wasn't a sign of a bruise or a scratch on him anywhere. I checked with the hospital and there was no record of an ambulance having indeed been sent out to Borthwick the previous night,' says Radcliffe, concluding that it had either been a monumental hoax, or something quite extraordinary.

Subsequently, it should be noted, Borthwick Castle has been exorcised.

Dominating the centre of Scotland's Capital City is Edinburgh Castle, a thousand years of history on a rock. If there is anything that symbolizes the passage of time and Scotland's greatness, this is the place. King Malcolm III and his Saxon Queen Margaret lived here in the eleventh century, after which it became a frequent retreat for the Scottish monarchy. After five centuries of attack by the invading English, it is remarkable that so much has survived. From the twelfth century onward, every occupant embellished the structure, so it is hardly surprising that there should be the occasional untoward event.

And no more untoward occurrence than that which took place upon a still and moonlit summer night over forty years ago when the guard at the gate was alerted to what sounded like the approach of a carriage

77

and horses. A loud clattering of hoofs could be heard coming from the cobbled path which slopes downhill from the great parapet of the Half-Moon Battery.

Edinburgh Castle has its own Governor, who is also the General Officer Commanding Scotland, and a contingent of soldiers is permanently in residence making sure of the castle barracks and officers' mess. On that particular night, there were eight soldiers in the guardroom, and when they stepped outside to see what was going on, they noticed that the castle gates had been opened. Now this was particularly odd since it usually takes at least two to four men to perform this task, which is very noisy, and yet there was no one to be seen.

And all the time, the sound of horses' hoofs grew louder and louder until there was a great surge of energy and something invisible, and very large, thundered past the soldiers and over the bridge as they stood in front of the guardroom door open-mouthed in astonishment.

All of this was noted down in the guard report for the next day, but when the commanding officer read it, he decided that it should go no further to prevent the regiment from becoming open to ridicule. So far as anybody knows, there has not been a repeat incident, or at least nothing that anybody is prepared to admit to.

With each of these incidents it is the 'time warp' theory that comes into play. What the puzzled onlookers are in effect seeing is a moment in time from the past which, in some sort of metaphysical response to something taking place in the present, undergoes an action re-play. It may take only one individual to trigger off the flashback. Alternatively, it might simultaneously come about in response to an event of some sort, a significant date in the calendar or the anniversary of some wrong-doing.

Whatever the reasons for such phenomena, it is important for us not to over-react and always to keep an open mind. In centuries to come, when mankind has come to terms with the potential of the human condition, all will most likely be revealed.

For Angie Passmore, such a revelation came entirely without warning when on holiday in the East Neuk of Fife. Married for seven years to Jack Passmore and living in Newton Mearns, in Glasgow, their marriage had reached a difficult stage when, in the absence of children, not to put too fine a point on it, they were becoming bored with each other.

The East Neuk was familiar territory. For

the third week in June, they and another couple had every year rented the same terraced seafront house in St Monans since their honeymoon. To begin with it was idyllic. Jack and Angie got on well with Richard and Diane Brown. Both couples liked the local hostelries, enjoyed the seafood, and while Jack and Richard played golf, Angie and Diane would drive in to St Andrews to shop, occasionally go to Perth or Dundee, or when the weather was good enough, just sit in the garden and sunbathe.

That was all very well, but in 1997 Angie suddenly tired of the routine. Richard and Diane rapidly realized that all was not well, and decided that the best thing for them to do under the circumstances was to make themselves scarce. So instead of playing golf one afternoon, Richard announced that he and Diane were off to visit Scone Palace and Falkland.

The night before Jack and Angie had had a monumental row over something totally trivial. And as a result, Angie was not at all happy at being left on her own with her husband. As soon as Richard and Diane had set off therefore, she went for a walk starting off along the shingle of the beach. It was a drizzly, blustery day, but that did not deter her. She must have walked for miles, climbing up and down the coastal path, over rocks on the shore, and then along sand before the sky suddenly became very overcast and there was a torrential downpour of rain. Noticing a small cottage with a light in the window, she ran up the pathway and knocked at the door. When a woman wrapped in a shawl answered, she asked if she could shelter there until the storm had passed.

The woman seemed nervous, but reluctantly agreed and motioned Angie to go and sit beside the fire. By this stage it had become almost black outside and Angie noticed that the cottage did not appear to have electricity. There was a large pot containing some sort of broth hanging over the open fire, and there was a strong smell of fish mixed with adours which Angie imagined to be a mix of earth and seaweed.

Time passed and the woman said nothing. Angie tried to make conversation, but the woman appeared not to hear her. She simply sat, wrapped in her shawl, staring out of the window. Angie could not help noticing how weather-beaten her skin was, and how shabbily she was dressed. In fact, the entire interior of the cottage was shabby. There were simple wooden stools and a basic table. Various bits of fishing gear hung from the rafters, and the floorboards were bare. 'I didn't think people still lived like this,' Angie thought to herself.

And then all of a sudden he arrived, a burly, bearded man with a face that looked as if it was lined with leather. He was wearing filthy oilskins off which the water poured in rivulets. It was obviously the woman's husband, for from the moment she heard his steps on the flagstones leading up to the doorstep, she became animated and let out a great cry of happiness. When he came inside, she flung her arms around him and the tears poured down her cheek. 'Hush, all's fine,' he said, or some such words as Angie says that the dialect was strange.

It was then that she noticed the sun was now pouring through the window glass. The storm had obviously passed, and so without ceremony she rose from the chair, thanked the couple as she stepped outside into the sunlight, and set off along the pathway in the direction of St Monans.

When Angie arrived back at the terraced house she had completely forgotten about the argument of the night before. All she wanted to tell Jack about was the strange couple and the cottage where she had found shelter.

However, Jack was incredulous. 'What do you mean there was a storm?' he said. 'The weather's been fine, not exactly blue skies, but it certainly didn't rain.'

'But it was pouring,' she protested. 'And the poor husband was soaked to the skin despite being covered with all that waterproof stuff.'

Such was her conviction that Jack decided not to press the matter further. That night he and Angie were as they had been when newly wed, and all the time Angie kept remembering the look of joy that had crossed the face of the strange woman at the sound of her husband's return. At breakfast the following morning she persuaded Jack and the others that they should come with her to see the cottage and its inhabitants for themselves.

'We'll take the car,' insisted Jack.

The fishing villages of Fife are located in easy reach of each other, and Angie knew that she had walked past both Pittenweem and Anstruther, but was certain she had not gone as far as Crail, although in the time she had taken she could easily have done so.

From the roadway it was soon evident that it would be pretty well impossible to work out exactly where the cottage had been, so when they reached Kingsbarns, the four of them decanted onto the beach and began the walk back.

It was another one of those days when the day started off grey, but then the sun came out and after a half mile, suddenly there it was, the cottage, but it was almost unrecognizable. For a start, there was no roof. The surroundings were overgrown and the window panes were broken and partially boarded up.

'I just can't believe it,' gasped Angie. 'That can't have happened overnight.'

Scavenging on the waterfront was an old man carrying a straw basket which he was busy filling with driftwood, so Angie immediately ran over to him to find out if he was a local. When he nodded, she asked him if he knew the folk who had lived in the cottage.

At this, he gave her a very long hard look. 'Naebody stays there onymair,' he told her. 'Not since Willie Sefton was lost at sea thirty years since. His wife Mora, she just upped and went. They were ae fond of ain anither. Most folk aboot here reckon she just upped and drooned hersel.'

Angie turned to have one last look at the cottage and without saying another word, she took her husband's hand. They set off back to the car in silence and a couple of months later, at home in Newton Mearns, Angie discovered that she was pregnant.

★ ★ ★

Hawick, as is evident from the story of the Silverbuthall Ghost, is a Borders town with a great sense of tradition. In 1815, what locals still call the 'New Road' to Carlisle was built. It replaced the old coach road which runs through Hawick, up the Howgate in the direction of the golf course, before branching along the hillside until it drops down to join the New Road.

Local historian Ian Landles is a mine of information on all subjects concerning his home town and its surroundings, and in the early 1990s, was contacted by a man who had recently moved to live in Hawick from Dundee. He wanted to know if Ian knew of anything strange about the old coach road and told him that he had been walking his dog one evening when he suddenly became aware of a presence. He had turned around to find a small green man with a hood looking at him as if to ask what he was doing there. The Dundonian had glanced anxiously at his dog to see how he was reacting, but when he looked back, the green man was gone.

The story, needless to say, took on a life of its own, and before long there were a number of sightings of this little green man, but Ian remained sceptical. Then he began to hear reports from the stables at Longbaulk, situated on the old coach road, that things were being moved around overnight and that the little green man was being blamed.

For many years, Longbaulk Farm had been lived in by Francis Henderson. It was a sad story since Henderson was Hawick's oldest living Cornet, having been the Principal at the 1922 Hawick Common Riding. This is the best known of the Borders riding festivals and takes place over two days in June. In 1929, for reasons unknown, Francis Henderson had fallen out with the Common Riding Committee and never attended the event again, although he did remember it in his Will when he died sixty years later.

Latterly, Henderson became a virtual recluse at the farm, but what started Ian Landles thinking about him was when a lady stopped him in the street one day to inform him that Francis Henderson's ghost had been seen wearing his green Cornet's coat. Shortly afterwards there was another sighting, on horseback this time, carrying his Cornet's flag and galloping along the old coach road.

Ian began to suspect that some inventive embroidery was going on, but not long afterwards another former Cornet told him of yet another encounter. This person had been driving his van up the old coach road in the gloaming and had noticed a boy ahead of him. From his manner he had assumed the boy was working a dog and, for a brief moment, he took his eyes off him to see where the dog was. When he looked back, the boy was gone. This astonished him since there was nowhere to hide, and he immediately stopped the van to get out and have a better look. There was nobody in sight.

What Ian instantly picked up on, however, was that the boy had been wearing a green coat, and this prompted him to call on the man from Dundee who had originally approached him.

'When you told me about the green man, you said you turned away from him to see how your dog was reacting,' said Ian. 'How did he behave?'

There was no reaction at all, explained the man, but added 'That was my new dog.'

Prior to the death of his old dog, the man from Dundee had often gone for walks on the same stretch of road and at a certain point, this dog had stopped and refused to move on. Each time, his master was obliged to pick him up and carry him for a few yards before putting him down. Afterwards, the dog would happily scamper on ahead and act normally, that is until they made the return journey. Always, it was at exactly the same spot that the old dog stopped in his tracks and refused to budge. And it was exactly the same spot where the van driver encountered the boy in the green jacket.

8

Graven Images

They were all kinds of colours,
Through this city
In their years,
The righteous, the ridiculous, the givers,
    and the just.
They scared us with its senses,
Made it giggle,
Dried its tears.
Until, into its quiet place, Glasgow wove
    their dust.

Unattributed verse featured in
The Glasgow Graveyard Guide, Jimmy Black

The nearest most of us consciously find
ourselves to the dead is in a graveyard, which
for many of us is too uncompromising and
sinister a reminder of our own mortality.
Cemeteries can be beautiful, which is what
they should be, but it is hard to resist the
macabre fascination associated with old
gravestones and the temples of remembrance
erected by those who have been left behind.

What is it then that makes us jump at the shadows? Too many *Dracula* films, or was it *Buffy the Vampire Slayer*?

It is the living's inability to come to terms with death that is compromised under such circumstances. There is nothing to fear from the remains of the deceased that lie at peace in holy ground unless, of course, their restless spirits are trying to tell us something.

Graveyards are where history is laid to rest. In Paris, there is Père-Lachaise, where can be found the melancholy footnotes of a multitude of legends ranging from the Scottish Jacques Etienne Macdonald, Napoleon's Marshal of France, to Oscar Wilde and the Doors pop singer Jim Morrison. Aside from being a focal point of French nationhood, Père-Lachaise has become one of the great visitor attractions of the twentieth Arrondissement. In Glasgow, on an equally impressive scale if not housing such high-profile residents, is the Necropolis.

In the early 1800s, Glasgow was a pretty unhealthy place to live. Approximately five thousand people died ever year from cholera, typhoid, and other diseases, and their bodies were mostly buried in pits behind the Old Royal Infirmary to the north of Glasgow Cathedral.

It was Dr John Strang, a historian and

one-time city chamberlain, who came up with the idea that Glasgow's well-to-do would endorse a last resting place in an open, leafy sanctuary. He recommended the Fir Park, a hill across the Molendinar Glen from Cathedral Hill.

There were few fir trees left on the hill. By then it had been transformed into a pleasure garden by the wealthy merchants of Glasgow. Lord Provost James Ewing liked his friend's idea and sold it to his merchant colleagues. A design competition for a new cemetery was launched and won by John Bryce who went on to create Scotland's first 'hygenic' graveyard.

Opened in 1831, Glasgow's Necropolis is an unashamed statement concerning the one-time wealth of the Second City of the Empire. Examples of virtually every kind of architecture in the world are represented, with a Jews' enclosure located close to Egyptian vaults and catacombs. Dominant over all stands a towering obelisk in tribute to the Protestant reformer John Knox, despite his being buried in Edinburgh.

I was first drawn to the Glasgow Necropolis for personal reasons. My great-great-grandfather was Peter Macquisten, a civil engineer and land surveyor, who in his brief career was associated with the building of several largely forgotten Glasgow master plans, and at the same time found time to father seven children. A protégé of Thomas Telford, the only surviving example of his work to my knowledge is the Macquisten Bridge over the River Cart on the Kilmarnock Road. The reason his name is not better known is that he was obliged to retire from practice in his late-thirties suffering from tuberculosis.

What strikes me as the most poignant chapter in Peter Macquisten's story is that towards the end of 1839, when he had become seriously unwell, he set off with his eleven-year-old son Patrick, his eldest son, to Pau, then a well-known health spa situated on the edge of the Pyrenees in Southern France. I have copies of the touching letters Peter wrote to his wife on the journey, describing the arduous coach trip, how they were robbed in Paris, and the relief he felt when they finally reached their destination.

In Pau, a few weeks later on 22 January 1840, at the age of thirty-nine, he died. Patrick, my great-great-uncle, was returned home, but it must have been a traumatic childhood for the boy who came home to discover that his one-year-old brother William and two-year-old brother John had both died of whooping cough since his departure. A year later, almost to the day, their seven-year-old sister Jessie also died.

And it is William, John and Jessie who were the first of the Macquisten siblings to be laid to rest in Glasgow's Necropolis. Their father was buried in Pau. Janet, my great-great-grandmother, must have been a resourceful woman to survive as a single mother in those days and still manage to put aside the money to buy the plots. She died thirty-seven years later at the Manse at Inverkip, where her third surviving son, Alexander, had become Minister, but she too is buried in the Necropolis.

Now all of this domestic history is inconsequential and only of real interest to family members. However, it does serve to focus the mind on this extraordinary citadel of the dead at the east end of Glasgow. Approaching the city by car, whenever I have caught a glimpse of it from Junction 15 on the M8 Motorway, I have felt a compelling urge to turn towards it.

And when I recently came across a collection of sepia photographs of Janet in her old age, the impulse became even stronger. When once more I found myself exploring the narrow footpaths that lead around and about and onwards and upwards to the summit, I began to understand why.

One of the most glorious symbols of Glasgow's past, something that looks as if it has been transplanted from another world in another dimension, from Gothic Transylvania even, has become a great, crumbling, vandalized mess. On the lower slopes, headstones are either broken or have toppled over. To be fair, the grass is cut, and the gates are now closed at night, but there is mindless graffiti and litter in all its forms liberally scattered all over the place. When I commented about this to one of the staff in the nearby St Mungo's Museum, he said, 'Yes, but you should have seen it before the last clean up.'

So why is this extraordinary sprawling statement about how Glasgow came to be the Second City of the Empire, European City of Architecture *and* European City of Culture being allowed to disintegrate behind its citizens' backs? And why is it that the living are so disrespectful of the past? Primarily it is because the living are more preoccupied with their own lives than those of ancestors they never knew. Secondly, it was created by wealth, and there are those who consider that any wealth that remains would be better deployed elsewhere to the living and needy and away from the self-indulgent, long-departed individuals who made it. Thirdly, there are very few of us who feel entirely comfortable about burial grounds.

Yet the potential is there for Glasgow's Necropolis to become as important a place to visit as the Arlington Cemetery in Washington or Highgate in London.

The work of some of Scotland's most renowned architects is represented — Alexander 'Greek' Thomson, David Bryce and Thomas Hamilton. On a plinth sits the Edwardian bleach tycoon Sir Charles Tennant, bearing an astonishing likeness to his descendants today. Sir Thomas Lipton, the tea importer and winner of the America's Cup yacht race, is here, as is a monument to the poet William Miller, author of the children's nursery rhyme 'Wee Willie Winkie'. These men were considered icons of their generation. They should not be forgotten, and some show of respect from the living would not go amiss. A start would be to tidy up their surroundings for them.

Now I am not sure whether it was my great-great-grandmother Janet or my great-great-aunt Jessie who sent me the subconscious summons to see for myself the state of their last resting place, but I have a lingering obsession that one of them had something to do with it.

When I reached home following my last

visit, I found one of the photographs of Janet had inexplicably found its way on to my desk top when I was certain that I had put them all away some time ago. I can only hope that by my writing on the subject, sufficient interest can be stirred up for somebody in authority to take the initiative and for something to be done about it.

Given the will, and a bit of love and attention, Glasgow's Necropolis ought to be recognized as a symbol of civic pride and as one of Scotland's most significant sites of historic interest.

Ten million bricks were used in the construction of Glasgow's City Chambers, officially opened by Queen Victoria in 1888. The lavish use of stone, marble and mosaic predominates throughout this Italian Renaissance palace which is still in everyday use as the city council's administrative headquarters.

Now with the opulence of the interiors and so much of Glasgow's history taking place within its walls, it might be thought that this would be the perfect backdrop for unexpected visitations, but over the past century there has been virtually nothing of a supernatural nature to report. That is until recently.

It was during the 1970s that Eric Hamilton

served as Lord Provost's private secretary, and was so highly thought of that following his death during the 1980s, a plaque was hung on the office wall in his memory. Two private secretaries followed him, but when Ian Easton took up the post in 1996, he decided that the plaque was not in keeping with the décor of the room, so he had it removed.

That was when the trouble started. One day Ian was sitting at his desk, which had formerly been Hamilton's desk, when it suddenly fell apart in front of him. On another occasion he was working late when the water machine in his room began gurgling and continued to gurgle. 'Usually it gurgles for a few seconds, a minute at the most, but this time it just went on and on,' says Ian.

At Christmas, prior to the Lady Provost's Christmas party for children, he had gone into the room in which all of the presents were stored. The light switch was on the far side of the room and having turned it off, he began to step carefully over the presents whereupon all of the toys that made noises started up. 'I left the room in a rush,' he says.

Then only the other day he noticed that the door to the Lord Provost's dining room was open. As he went to shut it, something persuaded him to step into the room to check it out at which point, the large central window suddenly blew open.

'It may sound daft, but I get the distinct impression that Eric Hamilton doesn't like me very much,' says Ian.

Not being liked can become quite a problem in Glasgow tenements when newcomers move into a street which has been occupied for several generations by the same families.

Although the English couple concerned with this story are anxious not to be identified, they are happy to put on record what happened to them when they rented a second floor, two-bedroom Victorian-built flat off Byres Road. John and his partner Alice are from Yeovil in Somerset, and when John was offered a job with an advertising agency located in Glasgow's West End it had not been an easy decision to up sticks and make the move. Happily, Alice, with languages and computer literacy skills, had already established a client base working from home. With a word processor and e-mail installed, it made very little difference where she was located.

And to begin with, they both liked the flat. There was a common stair lined with green and white wall tiles, and the accommodation was part furnished with polished wooden floors throughout. Within a month, shopping at Habitat and the Buchanan Galleries, with an excursion to Ikea, they had transformed it, introducing a variety of modern features such as scatter rugs, a glass top console table and a set of art deco prints to play down the rather dark and ornate Victorian built-in features.

And it was then that John and Alice decided to get to know their neighbours. Since moving in they had often encountered Jeannie Sinclair, an elderly lady, who lived on the first floor, and sometimes of an evening they had met Gus and Hannah McManus on the stair with their rather bad-tempered-looking son Pete. The McManus family lived directly above John and Alice and there were often shouting and banging noises late at night. In conversation with Jeannie, who preferred, as they say, to 'keep hersel to hersel', they discovered that the McManus flat had originally belonged to Hannah's mother Ina, who had passed away some years before. 'A cross old besom, but my best pal,' was how Jeannie described her.

With the best of intentions, John and Alice invited their neighbours to join them and a few of John's colleagues from the agency for a drink on Christmas Eve. It was an unmitigated disaster. To begin with, Gus and Hannah refused to drink champagne, and

John had to rush out to the nearest off-licence for lager. Then Peter McManus turned up from his work on a building site and it was obvious that he had already been celebrating the festive season with his mates. Not only did Pete throw up over the carpet but Hannah, who chain smoked, dropped a cigarette on Alice's brand new silk rug and before anybody noticed, it had burned right through to the varnish underneath.

'Never again,' agreed John and Alice when their guests had departed. But then later that night they were having a glass of red Burgundy together in the kitchen when all of a sudden Alice noticed that Jeannie Sinclair was still with them. She was seemingly asleep on the red rocking chair in front of the kitchen window, her head bowed and her hands folded over her lap. When Alice went over to wake her up, she discovered that she was dead.

It was all very distressing. The police and an ambulance were called, and Jeannie Sinclair was removed on a stretcher. The funeral took place a week later on New Year's Eve, and John and Alice, and the McManus family, were among the small contingent of mourners who turned up at the Clydebank Crematorium.

Immediately after New Year's Eve, John

and Alice went to spend a few days with Alice's parents in Somerset, and when they returned to Glasgow a week later, Jeannie Sinclair had already become a distant memory. That is until one afternoon, when Alice went into the kitchen to make a cup of coffee and clearly saw her sitting at the window on the red rocking chair. Moreover, she was not alone. Also seated, but on one of Alice's brand new calfskin kitchen chairs, was another woman with a wrinkled face, small beady eyes and a down-turned mouth. As Alice stared at them in amazement, they turned to look in her direction, then at one another, and then vanished.

When John came home from work, Alice did not know what to say to him, but eventually confessed to him what she had seen. Although sympathetic, he told her that she must have been imagining it.

Two weeks later, the incident occurred again, but this time to John. It was a Saturday morning and he had been working on the car. Instead of using the wash basin in the bathroom, he went into the kitchen and there, just as Alice had described it to him, were the two old ladies sitting at the window. Startled, he shouted at them: 'Get out!'

This time they not only turned to look at him before disappearing, but as they did so, a glass bowl was hurled at him which, missing his right shoulder, shattered against the wall. The crash brought Alice running, and when she was told what had happened, she exclaimed, 'Oh God! I don't think I can handle this any longer.'

Despite a For Sale/To Let sign over the stair entrance door nobody had, as yet, moved in to Jeannie Sinclair's flat on the floor below. That same night as the two of them lay awake in their bed, they began to hear the usual shouting and banging sounds coming from the floor above. Then all went quiet. Alice shifted under the duvet and noticed that John was sitting bolt upright in the bed. Against the window curtains, seemingly having a good old laugh with each other, were the two old ladies. And then John's favourite art deco print fell off the wall.

The very next day, John and Alice packed up their belongings and moved out. They now live in a modern apartment overlooking the Armadillo concert hall. 'I know it sounds comical,' says Alice. 'But it did happen. It really did.'

To the south of Glasgow, in Renfrewshire, on the Clyde coastline, is Inverkip where my aforementioned great-grandfather, the Revd Alexander Macquisten, was minister of the kirk until his death in 1906. On the outskirts of the village stands Ardgowan, ancestral seat of the Shaw Stewart family from the fourteenth century. The present large rambling house was built in 1791, and when Sir Houston Shaw Stewart, tenth baronet, brought his bride Lucinda to live there in 1982, she embarked upon a major redecoration of the old place, transforming it into a stylishly comfortable family home.

'When I started moving things around I stirred things up massively,' she admits. 'Of course, my husband's family have lived here for generations, so there were bound to have been some spirits left behind to keep an eye on things.'

While her husband has often seen apparitions in the house, Lady Shaw Stewart has only ever heard them, or noticed her dogs seeing them. 'A lot of people who have stayed here claim to have encountered sweet young servant girls wearing crossed apron strings, probably from the nineteenth century. And sometimes you hear this extraordinary noise as if there is a cocktail party in progress, which probably dates from before 1940.'

Ardgowan has one ghost who calls out names, which is very disconcerting for those concerned, and there is another one the Shaw Stewarts call the 'Happy Ghost,' who loves to join in when people are being entertained.

'One rather merry night there were twelve of us in the drawing room, and the piano played a chord all on its own. Everybody turned to look, but there was nobody anywhere near it. Another time we were all sitting up late and there was a terrible crash in the room, as if somebody had tipped over a pile of books. Again, nothing was visible and then, at dinner one night, a plate flew across the table.'

Lucinda Shaw Stewart is delightfully un-phased by such occurrences. 'It can be unnerving, especially late at night when you are on your own and hear footsteps and you wonder if somebody has broken in,' she says. 'But then there's nobody there and I always tell myself that if it is one of the ghosts, they've just as much right to be here as I have.'

She is far more concerned about the garden, which incorporates the ruins of an old chapel. 'A lot of battles were fought around here long ago and you can sense the melancholy and sadness in the grounds, but then you get that in a lot of places all over Scotland. It's all to do with the past never entirely letting go of the present.'

9

The Abbot House

When the children are playing alone on
   the green,
In comes the playmate that never was
   seen.
When children are happy and lonely and
   good,
The Friend of the Children comes out
   of the wood.

Robert Louis Stevenson,
A Child's Garden of Verses,
'The Unseen Playmate'

The Abbot House in Dunfermline's Maygate
is just a stone's throw from the great
Benedictine abbey founded by Alexander I of
Scotland between 1115 and 1124. As the
Church of Holy Trinity, it was raised to the
rank and dignity of Abbey by David I who
transferred to it a colony of Benedictine
monks from Canterbury in England.

With parts of the existing Abbey dating
from 1450, the Abbot Gaufrid arrived at the

earlier building in 1124, the first of a list of thirty-seven abbots and mitred abbots to the Reformation of 1560, then four commendators, all thought to have lived and died in the Abbot House. These powerful religious men also had houses in Perth, Stirling and Edinburgh. John Knox's House in Edinburgh, for example, belonged to Dunfermline Abbey pre-Reformation.

In 1618, John Taylor, the water poet, who in that year made his 'penniless pilgrimage' from London to Scotland, lodged at the Abbot House, as did Sir Walter Scott when in 1821 he was admitted as an honorary burgess of the Royal Burgh of Dunfermline. Over the centuries the Abbot House has accommodated both ordinary and famous folk alike.

In 1990, a group of local enthusiasts got together to form the Dunfermline Heritage Trust and set about raising over £1 million to transform the run-down premises into a local heritage centre. Little did they know of the forces they were uncovering as they set about their work.

Following the Reformation, the Abbot House was greatly altered and extended. At different times in its story it has served as a laird's mansion, an iron foundry, an art school, an orphanage, and latterly as a doctor's surgery. Using twenty Scottish artists and craftspeople working in metal, wood and stone, every room at the Abbot House tells a story relating to the period in time.

To add to the visual appeal, the exteriors were harled in pink, giving it the appearance of a large, pink-iced cake. Traditionally Dunfermline was known as the Auld Grey Toun, so why pink? 'Bull's blood,' explained Margaret Deans, a founder member of the Trust, and today Lord Lieutenant of Fife. 'That's where the colour came from in olden days, although we certainly didn't use blood this time. Long ago they had to use coagulated material to make the surface stick, and the poor bulls just happened to be available at the time!'

Inside, a life size figure recalls the presence of Robert Henryson, a fifteenth century Scottish poet who wrote *The Moral Fables of Aesop, Troylus and Cressida*, and various other works. He was a schoolmaster of the Benedictine Abbey School. Also to be seen is Lady Halkett, the seventeenth century herbalist who founded a school for the children of the Jacobite aristocracy, and Anna Munro, local born Scottish organizer of the Women's Freedom League. What the instigators of this paean to the past failed to anticipate, however, was that some of the other previous occupants might also want to muscle in on the act.

Sheila Pitcairn tells us that many Fifers admit to being 'fey' in the Scottish sense of the word, meaning that they have a heightened awareness of the spirit world. Sheila is a historian and has been closely involved in the development of the Abbot House for over ten years. This has enabled her to compile a mass of evidence suggesting that it is very much lived in by persons unseen and unknown.

The obvious candidates, of course, are the monks, and more than one visitor has commented on hearing the rustle of a robe and the flap of a sandal on the stairs. In 1992, an architect working on site claims to have seen vividly a figure in a habit emerge from one of the stones, and an archaeologist also working there suddenly felt so chilled to the bone that he was forced to leave.

The Queen Anne staircase in particular affects certain people. A former receptionist in the doctor's surgery recalled that when she worked there nobody could persuade her to go near the stairwell, and Sylvia Stewart, a member of the Abbot House staff, was on the staircase when she felt herself pushed from behind by an invisible force and broke her arm when she fell. A young boy, one of a group of youngsters with learning difficulties, refused point blank to go down them and had to be taken to another exit. Most people do not have a problem in managing the steps, but almost everybody comments on the sudden drop in temperature when they step out onto the landing.

In what is now the restaurant, one visitor recalled that he had been a member of Dunfermline Photographic Society based in the house during the 1970s. He was working in the dark room, which is now the Fire Room, when the lights failed and he ended up in the café area beside his father-in-law who was working at the sink. Both suddenly felt a drop in temperature, and then the very large, solid oak table in the centre of the room toppled over. Neither he nor his father-in-law were anywhere near it, and both felt the hairs rise on the back of their necks. Simultaneously, they hurried out of the place as quickly as they could run.

According to *Clark's Guide to Dunfermline*, 'The interior is divided into many small and some curiously constructed rooms, the kitchen having a stone-vaulted roof. The staircase is a narrow, winding stone one, and the story goes that some time ago, when alterations were being made, a skeleton was found built into the wall.' The ghost of a lady is also supposed to have been seen at the entrance to the old stone kitchen by a long ago servant.

Even the late Princess Margaret, Countess of Snowdon, sensed something untoward when she visited in October 1996. She refused to pose for photographs in the Radical Room because somehow it made her feel uncomfortable and the pictures were taken out-of-doors instead.

Nevertheless, Sheila is adamant that whoever it is who occupies the Abbot House means no harm since it is a house of goodness and love. She refers to a marketing meeting she attended with two gentlemen, one from Paisley, who afterwards announced that there were five to six bodies under the floor where they were sitting. When she explained that an archaeological dig was in progress, he said that they should go down a further five to six feet and the bodies would be discovered. He then explained to Sheila that he was a clairvoyant, whereupon she and her colleague Sheila Green invited him to tour the house.

'It was the experience of a lifetime because he told us many strange things,' she recalls. 'At every room he paused before he entered because he saw so many spirits who were all around us.'

His most thought-provoking revelation

concerned a room in the east tower. He described it exactly, having never been there, and when they came to it, pointed out that the treads of the spiral staircase were relatively un-worn, saying that it had been a one-way staircase. When they entered the room, he informed them that it was full of children.

Of course, it had been the bedroom where the orphan children and some of the adults were taken when they became ill and were expected to die. On repeating this story to Dr Jack Burt, whose surgery had once been held in the house, Sheila was told that this same room had been used in his day to store the practice's death records, and that it had been known as The Dead Room.

More often than not, it is children who see other children when adults are blind to them. Much is made of childhood innocence, but there is another avenue of thought which says that the nursery begins in the jungle. Playing wild in the woodland surrounding Fordel Castle, near Inverkeithing, a group of boy scouts on a summer camp recall a kindly old man giving them advice on which trees were safe to climb.

'It was odd really because we were told not to talk to strangers and our Scout Master was with us all of the time,' recalls Archie Wilson, now in his early twenties. 'He didn't seem to notice the man to begin with, and then one day he asked me to stop talking to myself. When I told him I was talking to the old wood man, he said not to be daft.'

It was then that Archie realized that the Scout Master had not seen the man, and if he was unable to see him, it therefore meant Archie must be talking to a ghost. 'But I knew he was for real. And my best friend George also saw him,' he says defensively. 'There was one time he took us to look at a tree house somebody had built. He had a beard and did look a bit like a tramp. He had this long coat and leather boots covered in mud, and he walked with a stick. It was a bit weird though. He'd just appear out of nowhere and then he'd just wander off and leave us without saying goodbye. I thought he must be something to do with the castle, but I never got around to asking him.'

Archie says he and his pals have never been back to the woods at Fordel since that summer back in the late 1980s. 'If he's still there I don't suppose I'd be able to see him now,' he says.

For almost forty years, until his death in 1995, Fordel Castle was occupied by Sir Nicholas Fairbairn, member of parliament for Perth and Kinross and one time Solicitor

General for Scotland. Sir Nicholas, a clever man with a brilliant wit, was a generous host, and the castle, a fourteenth century Scottish keep which he and his first wife lovingly restored, was his pride and joy. However, when guests came to stay, he also took great pleasure in warning them about Lady Pittodrie, a former mistress of the house.

Above a door in the drawing-room at Fordel is a witch stone which is said to have belonged to her, and what usually occurred was that those staying overnight would wake up suddenly to find that their bedclothes had been pulled off them. Curiously, this only took place when the guests were women. The men were never touched.

The Kingdom of Fife was ever a melting pot of Scotland's past, and close by Inverkeithing and Dunfermline is the Pitreavie Estate which in the fourteenth century was owned by Lady Christina Bruce, sister of King Robert the Bruce. By the start of the seventeenth century, the lands were owned by the Kello or Kellock family from whom, in 1608, they were purchased by Sir Henry Wardlaw for 10,000 merks Scottish. In 1711, Pitreavie House was bought by Sir Robert Blackwood, Edinburgh's Lord Dean of Guild, who transformed it from a fortified keep into an eighteenth century mansion. The

Blackwood family were a great naval family, one of whose number fought with Admiral Lord Nelson at the Battle of Trafalgar. In Edinburgh they are best remembered for having founded the literary *Blackwood's Magazine*.

The house remained with the Blackwood family for 170 years, although it lay empty for nearly a century. In 1884, it was bought by the Beveridge family who sold it to the Air Ministry in 1938 for the then enormous sum of £12,306.

In 1948, with the formation of NATO, Pitreavie Castle became the headquarters of the North Atlantic Area (HO Norlant) with the Air Marshal as Commander, Air Forces, North Atlantic, and the Admiral as Commander, Naval Forces, North Atlantic. This to some extent recognized the same strategic importance that made it so significant a location at the time of the English Civil War between Oliver Cromwell's Parliamentarian Roundheads and the Royalist forces supporting King Charles I.

In Scotland, of course, this was known as the Covenanters' War. Charles had decided that he wanted to bring the Scottish Church into line with that of England, and he had announced that the Scottish liturgy was to be revised, an explosively provocative gesture towards the Kirk. It was therefore not at all surprising that the Scottish Parliament backed Cromwell, but not all Scots agreed and religious conviction aside, many backed the King.

On 25 July 1651, Cromwell's army faced the Scots army on Castland Hill, close to where today's A90 becomes the M90. It was a rout. Towards the end of the battle, five hundred Highlanders were left to face the English alone with their backs to the wall of Pitreavie Castle.

The Wardlaws, who sympathized with Cromwell, showered stones and other missiles from the battlements onto the loyal warriors of Clan Maclean. Sir Hector Maclean and six of his sons died in the carnage, but before it was over a prophesy was made that for their infamy and cruelty, the Wardlaws would never again prosper, but pass 'like snaw off a dyke'.

Within eighteen months the first baronet died suddenly. Within fifty years the family fortunes ran out and the estate was sold.

With such hostility lingering on through the generations, is it any wonder that the melancholy grounds to the south of Pitreavie Castle are haunted by a headless Highlander who searches for his companions and is heard to groan and cry out whenever he comes across one of them dead or dying?

But within the castle walls itself, it is other long ago spirits that predominate. Manifestations often appear to show disapproval when there is a change of occupancy in a building. Over the decades, ladies in grey and green have been sighted by Officers' Mess members leaving the castle late at night, and in 1962, a cleaner was going about her business when she felt a hand placed upon her shoulder. Her initial reaction was that it must be a corporal from the guardroom with a message, but when she turned to find nobody there she fell into a state of panic.

On another occasion, a member of the WAAF is reported as having been hurled downstairs without any warning. More perplexing still, on several occasions the telephone operator reported that a number of calls were being made from an empty room. An Orderly Officer was sent to investigate and although totally unaware of it at the time, the operator later informed him that a call was made while he was actually in the room.

In 1999, Pitreavie Castle was sold by the Ministry of Defence and since 2001 it has passed into private ownership. Not much has been heard of late from those other unidentified inhabitants who walk the corridors and grounds, so one can only assume that they have found peace at last.

10

Experiences of the Spirit

Is there anything beyond? — *Who* knows? *He* that can't tell. Who tells that there is? He who don't know. And when shall he know? Perhaps when he don't expect it, and, generally when he don't wish it.

Lord Byron

On long term loan to the Smith Art Gallery and Museum in Stirling is a bronze bust of Callander-born Helen Duncan by the artist known as Dronma. Helen was a medium who gained an extraordinary notoriety for being the last person to be arraigned by the British Government under the 1735 Witchcraft Act as a danger to wartime security. Remember that at the time even Winston Churchill and Adolf Hitler were susceptible to stories of the occult, and when Helen informed a lady during a séance that HMS *Barham*, on which the lady's son was serving, had been sunk by the Germans, and that her son wanted to say

117

goodbye to her, it was too much for the authorities. HMS *Barham*, a Portsmouth ship, had indeed been sunk on 25 November 1941, but it was classified information. In a trial which Churchill himself branded as 'tomfoolery' and a waste of the nation's resources, Helen was hauled up before the Old Bailey and sent to Holloway Prison in 1944.

Mary Armour is the author of a biography of Helen entitled *My Living Has Not Been In Vain*. Inspired by Helen, Mary has been demonstrating as a medium for twenty-seven years, is President of The White Rose Fellowship in her home town of Gourock, and her work has taken her across the world from Iceland to Australia.

Mary has been receiving 'stuff' since the age of three. 'It's natural to you at that age,' she insists, but she was additionally fortunate in that her mother's life-long friend, her Aunt Jenny, was a medium and partly responsible for setting up the first spiritualist church in the Greenock area.

'Aunt Jenny often tried to persuade my mother to come along to meetings, telling her that she might get a message from someone, but my mother would have none of it. She did not believe in it right up until her death, but she didn't mind me becoming involved. Eight weeks after she died she appeared to me

118

during a Noah's Ark Society séance and I asked her if she believed in it now? She just laughed and said she didn't have much of an option.'

Mary is personable and relaxed about her gift. During her teenage years, the sense eluded her, but returned with a vengeance when she had a dream about a local boy called Eric Goldthorpe who, as it turned out, was a friend of her future husband. 'I saw him coming up Tower Drive on a motorbike and he hit a lamp post,' she recalls. Two days later the accident took place exactly as she had witnessed it in her dream.

On another occasion, she saw an aircraft sliding off a slipway, and a few days later the very same disaster took place, just as she had envisaged it, in Hong Kong. 'The problem with precognitive dreams is that you don't know where and when they are going to take place,' she says. 'That is why I believe in recording everything. All of my sittings are taped.'

For example, during a sitting in her hometown of Greenock, Mary said that she had a bad feeling about somebody and then asked, 'Who's Diana?'

'I know it sounds a bit absurd, but I replied that the only person I personally knew of with that name was the Princess of Wales. That was on the Thursday night and on the television on Sunday morning we all heard that she had died in that terrible car crash in Paris.'

That was back in 1997, and there is a record of the entire sitting on tape.

For all of her working life, Mary was a nurse, latterly working in intensive care units and involved in daily resuscitation. 'I have seen some really wonderful things,' she reflects. 'Patients talked of the land they saw while unconscious.'

Although heavily involved with spiritualism over the years, it is only since her retirement that she has been able to devote herself to it full time, travelling extensively to give sittings and lectures and to help those in need to make contact with loved ones who have passed over. Her early contact with Helen Duncan came about through the trance mediumship of colleagues, and she has no doubt that Helen chose her to write her biography. 'Coma, trance, dreams and hypnosis are all altered states of consciousness,' she explains. 'Coming back from the altered state of consciousness, sometimes the information comes flooding in. Helen has always been a great inspiration for me.'

Some years ago Peter McCue, head of the clinical psychology department at Ravenscraig Hospital, sent a memo asking for volunteers around the wards of the hospital where Mary was working. He wanted to find individuals willing to be hypnotized for research he was undertaking in his own time for a Ph.D. Degree at the University of Glasgow. 'He'll never be able to hypnotize me,' thought Mary, but applied all the same.

McCue's research was concerned with some assertions of the late Milton Erickson, an American psychiatrist and experimenter, pertaining to the nature of hypnosis. It did not have any direct bearing on the paranormal. A large number of subjects were involved in the research, and they did not all undergo the same procedure.

In Mary's case, he sat at a desk and invited her to sit on a chair in front of him and said: 'You're sitting on a chair on the lawn under a tree. It's a lovely sunny day. You can hear the church bells and the wings of the grey doves as they fly past. You can smell the roses.'

He paused for a moment, and then taking some keys from his pocket continued: 'When I rattle the keys you will cross the room, pick up the book on the table and place it on my desk.'

Mary remembers sitting very still, and then she heard him say, 'When I count from ten to one backwards, you'll open your eyes.'

So she opened her eyes, and he asked her how she felt.

'Warm and comfortable,' she replied.

Then he asked her if she thought she had been hypnotized, and she said no. The book was still on the table and she had not gone to fetch it when he rattled the keys.

That could well have been the end of the story, but two years afterwards Mary visited the spiritualist college as Stansted Hall in Essex. 'I looked out of the window of my bedroom and recognized the garden immediately,' she says. 'There was the lawn with the tree, and the flowerbeds were exactly as I had imagined them during the hypnosis session. There were grey doves on my windowsill, and on the Sunday morning I heard the church bells.'

When told about this, Dr McCue, currently Consultant Clinical Psychologist at the Anvil Centre in the east end of Glasgow, said: 'The things Mary recalls my saying were said after a hypnotic induction procedure containing suggestions for relaxation and hand levitation had been administered. I can't recall exactly what I said to Mary on that occasion, but I think she's wrong about doves — she might have thought of doves, but I'm pretty sure that I didn't mention doves, although I did mention birds.'

Over the past ten years Mary has done a lot of what she calls 'ghost-busting' after the popular Hollywood film. For example, there was a house in Greenock where the three young children were having a difficult time with sleeping. Mary took along her daughter Aily, who is a scientist, and they discovered that the children were being continually kept awake by unexplained noises. There was an unseen presence that could not be identified. 'I did the usual,' she says. 'I recited a simple prayer to make contact with whoever it was.'

She then explained that they would be safe if they walked into the 'white, bright light.' At that very moment, Mary felt a sudden powerful force push straight through her and out of the other side. When they played the tape back afterwards, there were a couple of loud bangs on the sound track. 'You simply have to make contact with the spirits and persuade them to walk into the light,' she says. 'Usually I ask them to leave a couple of raps on the tape to let me know they are going. Everything will then be all right.'

Mary is a member of the Scottish Society for Psychic Research, and is currently writing her second book on the subject of her own research. She is also in the process of setting up the Helen Duncan Foundation for the investigation of psychical phenomena under strict control provisions. In conclusion, she says she can relate to Bernard Carr, president of the UK Society of Psychic Research, who in a recent lecture observed that in his opinion, there are at least ten dimensions. 'Most of us are only aware of the one we are in,' she says.

It was a critical car accident in 1983, in which he nearly died, followed by the illness ME, that launched Grahame Wyllie on his spiritual journey. At the time he was living in Dundee and his quest began with automatic writing. The phrases: 'stop running' and 'face your fear' emerged. At the time prayer and automatic writing were the only connections he had in his search for fulfilment, but within weeks of leaving hospital he was talking to the light and hearing guides.

The full revelation came about a decade later just as he was preparing to go to bed. All of a sudden, he was aware of rings of purple light and found himself looking down on the earth, as if looking through a window in space. With him, he says, was a spirit guide who called himself Joseph of Aragon, and from that moment began Grahame's exploration of spiritual science, employing symbols and using energy chambers to reach higher dimensions. Now based on the South Side of Edinburgh, and accompanied by his partner

Fiona Mackenzie, he undertakes spiritual workshops throughout England and Scotland, with calls for advice coming from as far afield as Italy and Antigua.

Grahame and Fiona, a healer from Aberdeen, met on the Hebridean island of Iona and instantly became soul cousins. 'Everything I do has blossomed since we met,' says Grahame. They have lived in Edinburgh since 1998 and their joint-venture is called 'Iona Light — contemporary healing and spiritual technology for the twenty-first century.' They have a web site: www.iona-light.co.uk.

Fiona explains that she works with angels of 'The Elohim' who are higher beings from another universe, liquid light entities from spiritual realms in other dimensions. Together she and Grahame attempt to help people to move forward, people looking for a connection with another world, or who need help with personal growth.

At the same time, Grahame is continually aware of being surrounded by those spirits who have become trapped on this earth. Where possible he attempts to lead them to the light. 'Spirits recognize those who can help them,' he says.

For example, he and Fiona were on a visit to the Hermitage at Dunkeld with Grahame's three children. The kids were playing a game of tree hugging when one of them hid behind a tree, and yet Grahame still saw three children in front of him. And then he realized that there were others. They were rough but beautiful, barefoot and wearing sacking cloth. Fiona and his own children could not see them, but Grahame's children are very relaxed about their father's gift.

He explained to them and Fiona about the others and suggested a game of hide and seek. When one of the ragged children ran off down a path to the left and Grahame followed him, the spirit realized that Grahame could see him and seemed astonished. Grahame then asked the deva (spiritual guide), who was with them, if the children wanted to go to the light and when the answer was yes, helped them.

At Arbroath Abbey, Grahame was with a psychic investigation society on a visit to the Guard House when he realized just how psychically unaware his companions were. They had brought various pieces of equipment, lights and a tape recorder, with them but none of them were conscious of the ring of soldiers whom Grahame saw standing in a circle, swilling ale, joking, cursing and swearing.

Grahame asked the soldiers out loud if they

wanted to go home. 'You don't want to hang around here forever,' he said. One of them sat down in a chair and glowered at him while the others consulted with each other, then agreed. Grahame helped them, but the man in the chair remained adamant. He was not going to move.

Later in the day another psychic arrived, and the moment he entered the Guard Room, turned to Grahame and said, 'You've been doing some clearing here.' It was then that the remaining soldier changed his mind. 'I want to go,' he told them, and together they showed him how to run through the light.

Some months later Grahame met two women working as guides at Arbroath Abbey who told him how much more pleasant it had become for them. In the past, they said, there had always been the feeling that they were being watched and letched over by somebody or something. Now that sensation had gone entirely.

11

The Tides Return

Age on age the rocks remain,
And the tides return again;
Only we poor mourners, sinners
Weavers, toilers, fishers, spinners,
Pass away like visions vain.

Old Scots Song

Like many of my generation who grew up during the 1960s, I devoured the books of the otter man Gavin Maxwell, who remembered the above words from a song he had heard but was unable to give their provenance. A complex character, Maxwell wrote *Ring of Bright Water* and his later books at Camusfearna, the name he gave to his home on the west coast mainland of Scotland, opposite the Isle of Skye, at the head of Loch Hourn, which in the Gaelic translates as 'The Loch of Hell.' He later bought two lighthouse cottages on the Isle of Sandaig at the mouth of the loch.

During the 1970s, I was invited to stay on

the Kinloch Hourn estate, west of Invergarry. The lodge, as its name of Kinloch implies, sits at the head of the loch, but on my second visit I was quartered with friends in a two-bedroom cottage at Kylesmor which is half way up the loch, and only accessible by boat. The conditions were basic. There was neither tap water nor electricity, only paraffin lamps and candles, but the isolation was exhilarating. Without telephone or radio, there was virtually no contact with the outside world. We revelled in it.

When the sun shone, we all agreed that it was the nearest thing to paradise we had ever known. Like Gavin Maxwell, we swam in a waterfall, fished for crab in Barrisdale Bay, fed the midges, and trekked in the hills. Dinner at the lodge every night involved a five-mile boat trip with a hazardous return journey, steering by the reflection of the mountain on the loch surface.

When nightfall comes on the West Coast and the moon is veiled, everything becomes intensely black. For predominantly city dwellers, the experience of living the good life in such surroundings, especially travelling over water by boat in pitch darkness, was dangerous and exciting. At such times, the primeval nature of collective imagination runs riot.

A passage from Maxwell's *Raven Seek Thy Brother*, his last book, has always struck a chord with me. The title he took from an old Bedouin curse to annul the ill omen of sighting a single raven, and by this stage in his life, shortly before his death, he became convinced that he was jinxed with bad luck.

In the silver veil of island twilight, there are omens to be found everywhere. It is unlucky to hear the first cuckoo of the season before breakfast. Single cormorants, owls or ravens, in particular, are harbingers of doom. To meet a magpie in the morning is bad luck. A crow alighting on the roof of a croft presages a death therein.

But then omens, for those who believe in them, need not always be negative. The direction in which a bird chooses to fly can be of vital significance. The way in which the wind catches the flame or smoke from an open fire reveals all to those who know what to look for. The appearance of clouds against a blue sky, such as those at Athelstaneford forming the Saltire prior to the famous battle fought between the Northumbrians and the Picts c. AD 735. Superstition, in rural Scotland, and especially among Highlanders, has been rife for generations.

And almost certainly this is what drew Maxwell to the supernatural when at

Camusfearna he became preoccupied with the activities of a poltergeist. Not long afterwards he made the discovery that the abandoned lighthouse at Sandaig was haunted by voices late at night.

When Maxwell's friend, the writer Richard Frere, took up residence in one of the Sandaig cottages, he was woken up shortly after 3 a.m. and heard the voices moments later. 'The wind had dropped and it was raining. The voices, a curious disconnected muttering, rose and fell and seemed to be travelling down the north side of the house from west to east.' The sound, he wrote, suggested the passage of many people, and it went on for about ten minutes. Immediately afterwards, he fell asleep.

Highlanders allegedly attribute such manifestations to *taradh*, an influence exerted unconsciously by unduly strong wishes on the part of a person at a distance. Although Frere observed that the phenomenon never took place in stormy conditions, I too can vividly recall lying in my bunk at Kylesmor and hearing voices, but in the squall of the wind, and it was as if a great procession was moving past. Was it the deer coming down to the water's edge to drink? Was it a flock of geese flying low? I do not think so, and when I heard the sounds I had no intention of

131

getting out of my bed to investigate. Whether or not the two occurrences, less than ten miles apart, were in some way inter-related, is anybody's guess, but the coincidence certainly suggests an affirmative answer.

In the Hebrides, the mythical Land of the Spirit which the Celtic seers long ago named 'Tir nan Og' is ever present. Mirages are seen on days of heat and sea fog. The writer Adam Nicolson reflected that the deep past is more nakedly present than in any other place he knows, particularly in the Shiants, the three small, uninhabited islands he was gifted by his father when he reached the age of twenty-one, and which he has now passed on to his son at the same age.

The Shiants lie four miles off the east coast of Lewis, and the surrounding sea, Nicolson observed, makes you more attuned to habits and ideas that are unlike all the usual daily traffic of the mind. Sailing in his boat *Freyja*, and above all when out at sea late in the evening, he had only to look to the other end of the vessel 'for some other figure to be there, sorting out the ropes, wrapping the plaid around them'.

Throughout the Hebrides, from Islay to North Uist, superstition is rife, but it is a different sensibility to that found on the mainland. The isolation, the struggle against the elements, harshness of terrain, the vast emptiness of sea and sky, guarantees that. There is something about our primal conditioning that makes islands compelling. We see them from the prow of the boat, or look across at them from a cliff on the mainland, and we yearn to possess them. In the end, as Nicolson confirms, they possess us.

Shape-shifting, as it is known, is commonplace. A person is changed into an eagle, a dove or a white stag; sorcerers have the skill to transform human beings into ponies by shaking a bridle at them. Seagulls, in some instances, are thought to contain the as yet not fully departed souls of the dead.

The seas of the West Coast and far north of Scotland are a veritable aquarium of sea monsters, abounding in stories of seal men and kelpies, many of which at times verge upon the absurd. Believe them or not, the point is that usually great inventiveness is at play. Legends are passed down through the generations and are embellished to become folklore, the more eccentric the better.

On a calm night in 1748, while crossing the Busta Voe by boat, the four sons of the Gifford Family of Busta House were taken by seal men. The bodies of the boys were never recovered, and two hundred and fifty years on, the tragedy still resounds.

In North Uist, there was once upon a time a family called the MacCodrums of the Seals, traditionally descended from seals of the coastal waters. Certainly if you sail in the seas around Harris, Lewis and the Uists today, their heads pop up on every side to watch your progress. It is sometimes quite astonishing to see just how many of them there are, and how fearless they seem to be in such close proximity to human beings.

The story of the selkie of Suleskerry on Orkney is also well known. A young Orcadian girl fell for a seal man and gave birth to a child by him before he disappeared. Some years later, the girl came across a grey seal on the seashore and when it spoke to her, she recognized him as her selkie lover. Once again he vanished into the sea, but returned seven years later with a gold chain for her to give to their son.

The woman later married a local man, and years later her husband returned from a fishing expedition to announce that he had shot two seals, one old and one young. Around the neck of the young seal he had found a gold chain which he had brought back as a present for his wife. On seeing it, she realized at once that both her lover and son were dead.

The Sound of Shiant, off the east coast of Lewis, is sometimes known as the Stream of the Blue Men, strange, semi-human creatures, possibly kelpies (water horses), that prey upon passing boats. According to J. G. Campbell, author of *Superstitions of the Scottish Highlands*, one of these Blue Men was once captured by the crew of a ship and bound hand and foot. But his companions followed to save him and hearing their voices, with one mighty effort, he burst his bonds and was free. Were these simply the waves that he was referring to, or something altogether more fantastical?

In the majority, however, kelpies take the form of a black horse, having the ability to transform themselves into handsome young men when a young lady is present. There are numerous tales of such beings beside riverbanks and rock pools luring unsuspecting victims to mount them and be taken to a watery grave. Girls who are inclined towards the equestrian way of life should beware, although there have not been any reported sightings of this beast for some considerable time now.

Off Skye there are mermaids, known in the Gaelic as 'Maighdeans na Tuinne' (maidens of the waves). Gavin Maxwell told the legend of one caught by a Skye man in his nets. He took her home and when she shed her tail, he hid it in the rafters of his barn. They lived together as man and wife and she bore him many children until one of them came across the tail hidden in the barn and showed it to his mother. She grabbed it and without a backward glance, hurried down to the shore and was never seen again.

Tommy MacRae, a well-known head stalker on Lewis, had a story, hopefully tongue-in-cheek, about a stalking party setting out for the hill and coming across an old, old man on the pathway. His clothes were torn and tattered and he appeared to be starving, so one of the group, a city dweller overcome with compassion, handed him his lunch packet.

The day's sport was a disaster. The guns did not get within five miles of a beast and they were returning home disappointed when suddenly the stalker caught sight of antlers silhouetted against the skyline. 'Have a go at that one,' he told the city dweller.

It was a quick, clean kill and, as is the custom, the stag was gralloched on the hillside. Inside, they discovered the contents of the city dweller's packed lunch.

Whereas Hebridean mystical beasts tend to be confrontational, you tend to find that most Hebridean ghosts, as such, just like to be left in peace.

Perched on the shoreline of North Harris, with the main road running past its front door, is the large baronial edifice of Amhuinnsuidhe, built between 1864 and 1867 by the architect David Bryce for the seventhth Earl of Dunmore. The castle overlooks a secluded bay, but when the young earl took his English bride to see it she informed him that it was simply not big enough. An extra wing was then added, but by then the cost had escalated to such an extent that the family was obliged to sell the castle which then passed to a succession of owners. Among those who have stayed here was Sir James Barrie, the author of *Peter Pan*. His play *Mary Rose*, featuring a fairy island, was allegedly written at Amhuinnsuidhe in 1920.

Prior to that, however, in the late-Victorian era a servant girl called Milly came to work here and one afternoon, in circumstances unknown, she drowned in the Sound of Taransay. A carved stone on the water's edge commemorates this melancholy event.

More recently, the Amhuinnsuidhe estate was purchased by cider-heir Jonathan Bulmer and managed as a residential cookery, painting, and photography school, a superb location for those wishing to escape into the glorious Hebridean landscape and occupy their time usefully. The house is grand and welcoming, and nobody would even have considered the possibility of a haunting until Sebastian Bulmer, Jonathan's son, acquired a dog called Milly, and began calling out to her: 'Milly! Come here!' and 'Milly! Where are you?'

That was when it began. In a passage at the back of the house, painters in residence Tim Fargher and Hugh Buchanan, on separate occasions encountered a young girl who then vanished. In October 2001 the Dutch-Bolivian-American pianist Ana-Maria Vera, taking part in a series of evening concerts at Amhuinnsuidhe, was woken in her bedroom in the middle of the night by the passing shadows of a man and a woman. Everybody made fun of this afterwards, but Ana was adamant about what she had seen.

'Poor Milly. I think we must have disturbed her,' said Bridget Miller-Mundy, who at the time was responsible for organizing the courses and events at Amhuinnsuidhe. 'But at least we know she isn't unfriendly.'

On Mull, Julia Kileen, a painter, recalled her first husband Alasdair Macdonald telling her that he had seen the ghost of Old Ruaridh at Grass Point. It was the day of Winston Churchill's funeral in 1965, and Julia had been taken to hospital on the mainland for the imminent birth of her daughter Kirstie. Alasdair was hoping to get passage to Oban on the paper delivery boat which came into Loch Don. He had taken shelter inside the deserted Drover's Inn when, peering through the window, he saw an old man outside, quietly smoking a pipe and reading a book.

'Alasdair said there was something strangely peaceful about him,' said Julia. 'He banged on the window to find out if he knew when the boat was expected, but the old man ignored him. When he went outside, the old man was nowhere to be seen.'

Later, much later, Alasdair learned that the person he had seen was a well-known local character who had died some years previously. In his declining years there was nothing Old Ruaridh enjoyed more than taking a book to read on the shore of the Firth of Lorne — and he hated to be disturbed.

Island life in the Hebrides is conditioned by the weather and, more often than not, there are five types in a day — rain, wind, sunshine, mist and snow. From the lush and overgrown landscape of Mull to the desolate, peat-sodden moors and hills of Lewis, beliefs are inextricably bound up with the stark reality of everyday existence. Since the terrain is timeless, it is not unrealistic to believe that the shadows that stalk the land are of a greater antiquity than those that are prevalent elsewhere.

So when the wind howls or when the clouds hang low over the horizon, strange sounds creep eerily into our subconscious thoughts and fears as they did with our ancestors a thousand or more years before.

Robert Loudon, an apprentice architect, was driving along a track on Islay late one evening on his way to meet some friends who had arrived off the afternoon ferry at Bowmore. Having consulted his map, he had taken a turning expecting it to be a short cut, but soon found himself surrounded on all sides by desolate moorland and an occasional lochan.

It was becoming dark when, on the shore of one such pool of water, he spotted an old woman dressed in rags who appeared to be washing some clothes. He pulled over momentarily to check with her that he was heading in the right direction. She was obviously startled because she leapt around to face him and when she did so, he was so utterly repelled by her gnarled and hideous appearance that he at once slammed his foot down on the accelerator and drove away at speed.

He had gone no more than a mile when the

car blew a gasket and steam began to pour out of the bonnet. Not willing to walk the remaining distance, he topped up the radiator with a can of water he had kept in the boot of the car and carried on regardless. Eventually, he reached a main road, whereupon he pulled the car into the side and waited in the dark to be rescued.

'You were lucky,' he was told later. 'What you saw was the 'bean-nighe' or 'washing woman'. Most people who see her do not live to tell the tale.'

Tradition has it that the old lady would have most likely been washing and preparing the shrouds of those who were expected to die. The reasons that such a remote spot was chosen for this was so that nobody might see her. Apparently, Robert had a lucky escape because he had seen her before she saw him.

Should the 'bean-nighe' be caught in the act, her vengeance is allegedly terrible. There are some, however, who say that she means no harm. Indeed, it is also said that if you can get between her and the water, she will become your servant and tell you all you wish to know. Notwithstanding, Robert was simply relieved to hand his car over to the Automobile Association and to catch up with his friends, who, as one might have expected, dined out on the story for weeks afterwards.

12

Primrose's Story

Some places speak distinctly. Certain dank gardens cry aloud for a murder; certain old houses demand to be haunted; certain coasts are set apart for shipwreck.

Robert Louis Stevenson,
Memories and Portraits

The Glasgow-based newspaper journalist Fidelma Cook has a reputation for her astutely researched and uncompromising interviews and features in the *Mail on Sunday*. In 1989, she and the photographer Dave McNeil were sent to Edinample Castle, on the south side of Loch Earn, which was undergoing restoration by the architect Nicholas Groves Raines. The castle was in the process of being meticulously restored to its former glory, and as Fidelma was being given a conducted tour by Nick and his wife Limma, it suddenly felt as if somebody was pushing her. Shown into what was designated

1. The entrance to the underground Goblin Ha' at
Yester Castle

TRADITION SAYS THAT
THIS IS THE GRAVE OF
DAVID RICCIO 1533-66
TRANSPORTED FROM
HOLYROOD

4. Alanna Knight, who has known from childhood that she has psychic awareness

2&3. (left) The grave that is said to be that of David Riccio (1533-66), Mary Stuart's murdered secretary

5. Borthwick Castle, a superb example of the Scottish fortified house

6. The Abbot House, Dunfermline, haunted by monks – its former occupants

7. The Necropolis, Glasgow, with its monuments to the past glories of the Second City of the Empire

8. Grahame Wyllie and Fiona Mackenzie who believe that they are led by spirit guides

9. The five cylindrical stones on top of the grave of Seath Mor Sgort Fhiaclach, a chief of Clan Shaw

10. Swein McDonald,
The Highland Seer

11. Laurence, Jenny
and Charles Blair
Oliphant at the
entrance to Ardblair
Castle, the scene of
inexplicable encounters

12. Playwright and author A.J. Stewart, who discovered that she had been born and lived 500 years ago as James IV, King of Scots

13. A portrait of James IV of Scotland aged 40

14. Craigmillar Castle where the ghost of a black horse has been regularly seen

15. Sir Iain Noble exploring the remains of one of the six fairy houses in Gleann an Uird on Skye

to become a child's bedroom, the tension increased, almost to the point of panic. Later when she sat down to lunch, Fidelma asked Nick and Limma if there was something she should know about the old place. Glancing at his wife, Nick then proceeded to tell them the story of the builder of the original keep, Black Duncan of the Cowl.

Duncan Campbell was aged forty when he inherited substantial lands from his father Grey Colin, sixth Laird of Glenorchy, who had ruthlessly seized them from Clan McGregor. Black Duncan, as it turned out, was far greedier and more unprincipled than his father, and through marriage and deception soon added Menteith, Glendochart, Glenlochy, Glen Falloch, Glen Lyon and Lorn to his landholdings. All of his life was embroiled in plots of one sort or another: an attempt to poison his cousin, the Earl of Argyll, and the murders of both the Earl of Moray and of Campbell of Cawdor. Yet through friendship with King James VI, he escaped prosecution.

In the early seventeenth century at Edinample, Black Duncan instructed his Master Mason to build a walkway around the battlements so that he would be able to view his lands on all sides. This was done, but when it came to inspecting the final results,

Duncan tripped and fell and this so enraged him that he pushed the unfortunate Master Mason over the battlements to fall to his death in the moat below.

All of this was far removed from the interiors feature that Fidelma and Dave were working on at the time, but when Dave's photographs were processed the following morning in Glasgow, a sinister, cloud-shaped shadow was evident hovering in the background of all of the pictures. Although the article was published later that week, the negatives and all copies of those photographs have since unaccountably disappeared.

When Brendan Murphy, a sociology academic from Hull University came to Scotland during the 1980s, he launched WorldWright Communications, a media publishing company, based in Aberfeldy. At the same time he began the restoration of an old house called Achloe at Fortingall, on the edge of Glen Lyon. Renovating the building was a major challenge and while work was in progress he received a visit from a former colleague from Sheffield who some years before had gone to live in the West Indies.

At the time, there was no mains electricity in the house, only well-lit oil lamps giving off a very clear, white light. Brendan recalls welcoming his friend and sitting him down at a table with a bottle of Golden Rum. 'We had a lot of catching up to do,' he said. 'Then this casually dressed young girl with long hair came into the room and joined us. There was nothing particularly striking or extraordinary about her and I simply assumed she was with David.'

Thinking back on it afterwards, Brendan cannot recall her saying much if anything, just sitting next to them smiling and occasionally nodding her head. Then quite suddenly she got up and walked out through the door at which point David asked Brendan who she was.

He had assumed she must be a neighbour or some sort of relative.

'When I told him I had no idea, he freaked!' said Brendan. 'I had assumed that the lass was with him.'

In Jamaica, David had been exposed to all sorts of weird things such as voodoo and thought he had left it all behind him. 'And just in case you are wondering, neither of us was smoking any hallucinatory substances,' insisted Brendan. 'It really was a very strange shared experience which neither of us is likely to forget.'

Glen Lyon is rather famous for its unexpected visitors. During the 1980s it was quite usual for Hogmanay revellers in the district to first foot each other after the bells, and the common practice was to leave the door open with bottles and glasses set out on the kitchen table so that anybody who dropped in could help themselves. At Ardtrascot, on the Clachan of Ben Lyon, there are several locals who vividly recall seeing a large jolly man sitting in a chair and drinking steadily over a time scale of several hours. He wore an old-fashioned tweed coat and seemed perfectly at home, occasionally shifting a log onto the fire.

A sociable community, it is curious that nobody remembers actually speaking to him. All the same he appeared to be having a good time on his own until the owners returned, when he disappeared. Nobody has seen him since and nobody has the slightest idea who he was.

For several years during the late 1980s, the garden designer and author Suki Urquhart lived in a sixteenth-century fortified mansion house in Banffshire. The house was built around a courtyard, and when Suki first moved in, she decided to make use of a wing off the front hall. After only one night of sleeping there, or rather not sleeping there, she decided to move to a room in the other wing.

'I kept being woken up by something,' she

recalls. 'It sounded like a child crying, and then it became an elongated sigh. It really unnerved me.'

Later, while researching the history of the building, Suki discovered that it had long ago been occupied by the Duff family. Captain George Duff was killed at the Battle of Trafalgar in 1805 when his head was blown off by a cannon ball as he leant over the side of the ship. Admiral Norwich Duff also served at Trafalgar, fought in the attack on New Orleans, commanded the *Espoir*, the *Beaver* and the *Rifleman*, and found time to father eight children.

He was most likely playing safe. In an earlier generation there had been an outbreak of scarlet fever and the Duff of the day had walled up his wife and daughter in quarters off the front hall, feeding them through a window until they were no more. Some local people who had known this story prior to Suki's arrival told her that for centuries that side of the house was always referred to as the 'Fever Wing'.

The house was sold to friends during the late 1990s, and more recently Suki was invited back to stay the weekend. By then, she had forgotten all about the Fever Wing, but on her way upstairs to her room, and later on her way to the drawing room having changed for dinner, she passed the passageway leading through the kitchen to that side of the house. Very clearly she could hear voices talking loudly to each other. Over dinner, she asked her hostess if a television had been left on.

The answer was no, but not long afterwards she was told that the Catholic owners of the house had asked for an exorcism.

Aberfeldy-based James Irvine Robertson, a broadcaster with Radio Heartland, and author of a string of historic novels, has come up with a curious tale concerning a family who lived at Old Blair, in Perthshire, for many years the factor's house of Atholl estates. Prior to that it had been an old coaching inn.

When she and her husband first moved into the house, says Irvine Robertson, the mother was told that it was haunted, but had decided not to tell the various members of her family. Then one night her daughter had a particularly vivid dream in which she saw herself step out of bed and open a large walk-in cupboard in her bedroom to find a lady dressed in grey sitting there. She immediately retreated to her bed and was followed by the grey lady who began to shovel coal on to the pillow.

When she told her family about it the

following day, her mother was inclined to dismiss it simply as a nightmare. However, it did occur to all of them that the bed head in the room had been pushed up against a blocked fireplace.

Time passed, and Aunt Primrose arrived for the weekend from London accompanied by her future husband. Relatively tired following the long journey, the couple retired to bed early, but in the middle of the night Primrose awoke to find her betrothed thrashing about beside her, obviously having a nightmare. She sat up and, in the half-light, saw a woman dressed in a black gown standing at the foot of the bed. Primrose said afterwards that she felt no fear, but was nevertheless convinced the figure was male-volent. As she watched, it turned to move slowly away from the bed and slid behind a curtain.

Straight away, Primrose turned on the light and dug her man in the ribs. He was in a bit of a state, not least because he had taken rather more Scotch than was good for him after dinner. Nevertheless, he told her he had been dreaming about a woman in black intent on doing him grievous harm. He had actually been in the throws of defending himself against her when he woke up. His struggles had been a desperate attempt to prevent himself from throttling her. Immediately before he came round, he said, the woman changed into a black cat, which admittedly does sound a bit over the top.

Primrose's story, however, rang a faint bell with Irvine Robertson who was sure he had come across something similar in the great pile of family documents he had inherited from his father. In the century before, James's great-great Aunt Sophia had been married to John Robertson, the Atholl factor, and they had lived at Old Blair for fifty-three years. In one of the boxes stored in the attic James eventually unearthed a document handwritten by Jane, Sophia's niece, in 1920.

In this she recorded that although her aunt had told her that she had never seen an apparition herself, Mrs Forbes, her successor at Old Blair, had been recovering from influenza and was sleeping badly when:

> Suddenly she noticed standing near the foot of her bed the figure of a woman dressed in grey. As Mrs Forbes looked, the figure moved a little, then disappeared . . . She asked Mr Robert Inglis, the assistant factor, if he had ever heard that Old Blair was haunted, but did not tell him of her dream. He said that he would ask from his landlady (in Bridge

of Tilt) who knew all the old stories of the district.

Mr Inglis's landlady was named Stewart, the sister of Sandy Stewart at the front lodge and she lives in Tilt Cottage next to Corner House. Next day he brought the information that Old Blair was indeed haunted by a grey lady, that the Macduffs had seen her, and others before them, but she had never known it to appear in the Robertsons' time.

Jane confirmed that it had been Mrs Forbes herself who had told her this tale while driving back from a lunch party at Calvine in the summer of 1906.

There is also a postscript to Aunt Primrose's ordeal. Following her visit, a canon of the Church of England came to stay at Old Blair, bringing with him a small bottle of water he had taken from a well sacred to St Alkmund in Derbyshire. At breakfast his hostess asked him how he had slept. Fine, was his well-mannered reply, but then apologetically went on to confess that to tell the truth he had at first sensed something most sinister in the room. Uncapping his bottle, he had sprinkled holy water across the bedspread in the sign of a cross, something he had never done before.

The sign of the cross, however, is not always a fool-proof device for deflecting evil. Sometimes it can act as a catalyst to reveal an ancient wrongdoing. When Katie Sondal, a senior executive with a fabrics marketing company based in the Borders, sought solace and escape from a broken marriage in a converted farm steading near Montrose, she was at first enchanted by the place. It was almost Elizabethan in appearance, with large interior ceiling beams, and oak panelled walls. 'It must be very old,' she remarked to her landlord, who lived nearby, and was amused when he replied, with honesty she thought, that she should not be fooled by appearances.

Whether the steading was old or not, was unimportant. Close by was the North Sea, and inland there was rich farmland providing some glorious walks to be enjoyed along rustic footpaths. This was just the tonic she needed; it was the opportunity for her to clear her mind of all the hurt and baggage of the past.

For a fortnight's let, the kitchen was exceedingly well furnished with every modern convenience. In the upstairs sitting room the chairs were chintz covered, and in the bedroom, which was on the ground floor, there was a four poster bed with silk hangings. It was rather grand, thought Katie, dismissing how out-of-place it was.

However, she was not so certain about the four wooden crosses that hung from the pelmets on each corner, but concluded that the family to whom it belonged must be deeply religious. She also noted that there was a crucifix on the far wall. Although a churchgoer herself, it was not the décor she would have chosen, but all the same, she did like the idea of sleeping in a four poster.

And she liked the idea even more when exhausted from the trip north, she climbed into the sheets around 9 p.m. She had been sleeping badly of late, so it would have come as a merciful relief, had she been conscious to recognize it, when she fell almost instantly unconscious. Yet the dreams were so vivid.

To begin with, Katie saw herself in a beautiful wood. All about her was a carpet of forest flowers, and she was not alone. There was a man with her — tall, dark and handsome, like some hero in a Barbara Cartland novel. She felt overwhelmingly happy, and then, quite suddenly, the mood changed. The wood became dark and sinister and the man turned violent, striking her to the ground and forcing himself upon her. Katie screamed and woke up.

The illuminated dial of her travelling clock told her that it was 2.30 a.m. She turned on the bedside light and everything looked normal. The curtains were drawn and the house was silent. There was only one thing untoward, and that was an almost over-whelming smell of wet soil. It must have been raining, she told herself, and turned off the light to go back to sleep.

A week later, the cure was beginning to take effect. The sun had shone constantly day after day, and the pure air of the sea was working on her like a tonic. Each day she had planned a different excursion. She had taken the car to go shopping in Arbroath and Brechin, and gone to visit Glamis Castle, the childhood home of Queen Elizabeth, the Queen Mother. On other days she had simply made up a picnic and gone for a walk or sunbathed in the garden. She revelled in the solitude. This was heaven, except for the nights.

Three times she again had the same dream about the wood and the man, and had woken suddenly to smell the damp earth. She told herself it must be some metaphor relating to her past. It would get better, and besides, the smell was only part of the dream. During the day, the bedroom smelt fresh and clean. When she went out she left the windows open, just in case, reflecting on how wonderful it was to be in such a place where one was able to do so without fear of burglary.

And all too soon the sunlit days came to an end, and Katie knew that she would be returning home to face up to her future. The evening before her departure, the landlord and his wife invited her over to the farm for a drink.

The farmer's wife was a large, jolly woman in contrast to her rather dour husband. 'We're sorry we haven't seen more of you,' she informed Katie. 'But we got the impression you wanted to be left alone.'

She was fishing, thought Katie, but then decided, since she was leaving, that there would be no harm in filling her in. 'I'm recently divorced,' she explained. 'I just needed some space to get my head together.'

'Men,' said the farmer's wife sympathetically. 'Can't live with them. Can't live without them.'

And then she suddenly turned serious. 'And how did you find the steading? Were you comfortable? Did you sleep well?'

Katie nodded. 'Yes, very well, except . . . '

She paused. The farmer's wife looked anxious.

'Well, I did have this odd recurring dream

about walking in a wood,' she said. 'And then when I woke up there was a horrid smell of earth. But don't worry, it was just a dream and the smell was always gone in the morning.'

The farmer and his wife exchanged what appeared to be nervous glances and changed the subject.

That night the dream recurred again, only this time the smell of earth when Katie woke up was even more pungent than it had been before. Again, it was 2.30 a.m., and this time Katie got up to go to the kitchen to make herself a cup of tea. Everything was very, very still and despite it being a warm night, she shivered as she poured the water from the electric kettle into the mug and took it upstairs to the sitting-room.

It was then that she noticed for the first time the watercolour painting over the fireplace. Katie recognized it immediately as the copse in the wood in her dream. Examining it more closely, she saw that it was signed and dated — Margaret Lumsden, 1938. The farmer's name was Lumsden, so presumably the artist must have been a relative. Katie resolved to ask him about the picture when she went to say goodbye in the morning.

However, when she had packed up her

bags and taken the steading keys to the farmhouse door, it was the farmer's wife she saw. Seizing her moment, Katie asked her about the painting and told her about the dream. The woman crossed herself.

'We didn't want to tell you and we thought that you'd think it was nothing,' she began. 'Margaret Lumsden was my husband's aunt, a very arty lady who spent most of her time travelling — Paris, Rome, Vienna, all those arty places. There was no shortage of money, and it was her idea to convert the steading.

'She was a right fancy woman and led the men on something rotten. There was this good looking lad up from Glasgow who did joinery work to earn a living, and she took him on to fix the floors and panelling. That wasn't all she took him on for, mind.'

Mrs Lumsden paused nervously, then continued. 'I wasn't around in those days, but you hear talk and the story I heard is that they had a favourite place in the woods they used to go. Margaret might have played fast and loose when she was away from home, but she didn't want her father to catch her at it. The old man had a real brute of a temper when aroused and he was always on at her to make an honest woman of herself. The problem was that she'd come into money of her own from her mother's sister, so after that she reckoned she could do what she liked and she told him so. Then one day she just upped and went.'

'She went away?'

'That's what they say. She just wasn't around any more. Her dad just said she'd taken herself off to one of those arty places with some of her well-to-do friends. Then the war broke out and well, everything changed.'

'What happened to the joiner?'

'Oh, he finished off the work, must have put down the floors just about the time she took off. From what I was told, he went back to Glasgow, got called up into the army and was blown up in a trench somewhere in France.'

'And your husband's family never heard from his aunt again?'

'Never, except . . . '

'Except, what?'

'Except there are those who say she's been seen at the steading. I wouldn't have told you, except that you're going now. Some folk we've had there to stay say they've seen her, or somebody, mostly late on at night.'

'The crucifixes on the bed? Do they have anything to do with it?'

'That was the bed the old man slept in. It was said he never again had a decent night's sleep after she left. We moved it there from the farmhouse after he died. I sewed the crosses on it myself.'

Katie shuddered at the thought of it. Presumably the old father had died in that bed and she had been sleeping in it. She was glad she hadn't known at the time. 'Has anybody ever said anything before about the smell of wet earth?' she asked.

Mrs Lumsden looked embarrassed and nodded. 'You mightn't have noticed, but that's why my husband came over all funny last night after you'd mentioned it. You mustn't tell a soul, but he reckons that either his granddad or the joiner lad did for her, and she's under the floor. Either that or she's in the woods, some place.'

Katie returned home that day confused, her own problems dismissed from her mind. A month later she received a letter from the farmer's wife to say that they had finally bitten the bullet and taken up the floorboards at the steading. Immediately below they had found an earth floor but instead of the surface being dry and crumbly, it was packed solid and was as hard as concrete. Scratched on the wall in mud very indistinctly they discovered the words, 'Help me!' That did it, the Lumsdens had decided to level the building.

13

My Lady

Divinity or Theology, as it proves the existence of a Deity, and the immortality of souls, is composed partly of reasonings concerning particular, partly concerning general facts. It has a foundation in *reason*, so far as it is supported by experience. But it is best and most solid foundation is *faith* and divine revelation.

David Hume, *An Enquiry Concerning Human Understanding*

In the late 1980s, Fidelma Cook and her family moved to live at Gartloaning, a seventeenth-century farmhouse constructed on an ancient ley line near Aberfoyle. It was one of those traditional houses built with a staircase positioned immediately in front of the front door, but subsequently there were extensive alterations. Two centuries later, the staircase had been turned and the front entrance re-positioned.

Although Fidelma never actually saw the apparition herself, it was not long before her mother, who had come to live with her, started seeing an elderly woman with full skirts and an apron, her hair neatly tied back in a bun, who came down the stairs that were no longer there and passed through the door that was no longer there. Fidelma's four-year-old son Pierce also spoke of 'My Lady', who used to visit him in his bedroom and tickle him during the night. Sometimes, when Pierce's nanny was downstairs, there would be a sudden rush of air and she would sense the swish of skirts as somebody moved past.

'Oh, that'll be Old Mary,' Fidelma was told by an octogenarian man in the village who first visited the farm when six years old. Apparently Old Mary was well known in the locality.

In 1991, Fidelma's mother suffered an aneurysm and although reluctant to have the operation, agreed to go into hospital where she died some days later. Afterwards Fidelma had a visit from the previous owner of the house, a family friend, who told her that her mother had confided in her that she would not be returning home. Shortly before she had left the house for the last time, she had seen Old Mary again, but this time instead of moving down the staircase and out of the door, Old Mary had been cleaning. As she progressed through the kitchen, dusting and sweeping as she went, she had suddenly turned to look straight at Fidelma's mother who had known immediately that her time was up.

★ ★ ★

Much consternation was stirred up in May 2002 when it was suggested that an exorcist should be employed at the Tolbooth Theatre in Stirling. This followed the £6 million renovation of what used to be a former jail. Employees claimed to have seen wine glasses fly off tables and door handles turn without human hand in the theatre restaurant which is located in the part of the building where once prisoners were housed awaiting execution.

According to operations assistant James Wigglesworth, the building is totally transformed from its original purpose, but a lot of strange goings-on had taken place. Late at night he had heard all manner of things going on in the old cells upstairs, and had heard what sounded like a body being dragged across the floor. In another incident, a barman in the cellars found the doors of a spirits cabinet shaking violently. When he opened the doors to see what was going on, bottles fell out and smashed on the floor.

One explanation proffered is that during the conversion of the category A-listed building, a skeleton was found. This was later identified as Allan Mair, a murderer who was hanged outside Stirling Tollbooth in 1843 after he bludgeoned his wife to death. The skeleton was discovered by builders when they lifted the concrete floor close to the prison entrance. It was almost intact in the coffin in which it had been placed over 150 years before, and he was still wearing his boots. Although he was subsequently given a Christian burial in January, a postman delivering mail to the building is convinced that a figure in nineteenth-century costume passed by him through the door and said 'good morning,' before disappearing.

Karl Kirkland, assistant bar and restaurant manager at the Tolbooth Theatre, was reluctant to walk alone in certain parts of the building after he noticed that the gas in the cellar kept being turned off when there was nobody else around. To begin with he thought that somebody was just having fun, but it took place once too often.

Stirling's Tolbooth Theatre has an obviously sinister past as an old building that has witnessed great stress and malevolence. Other properties, however, are more likely to keep their secrets to themselves, that is unless somebody accidentally stumbles across them.

Another example of a hanged man seemingly determined to make his presence felt appears to have been experienced by Elizabeth Salvesen, whose family moved to live in the Midlothian village of Ratho in 1956. Their house was built into a hillside, and Elizabeth's bedroom was on the first floor, level with a cinder path in the garden outside the window. From her very first night there, at the age of nine, she began to hear the crunch of footsteps on the path.

For eight years she was told not to worry, that she was simply imagining things, and then on a Saturday in 1964 the *Scotsman* newspaper published an article on George Bryce, hanged in 1864, the last man to be publicly executed in Scotland. The feature did not name the house where the crime took place, but the description was extremely familiar. When Elizabeth's parents questioned the daily help and gardener, they confirmed the story, explaining that they had not told them before because they had thought it would only frighten them.

George Bryce had lived in the village a hundred years before and become obsessed with Jane Watt, the nursery maid who lived at the house which then belonged to Robert Todd, a mill master and grain merchant. To begin with Jane had encouraged George, but was warned off by the cook who told her that he was a bad lot.

Poor, unfortunate Jane. Very early one morning her suitor turned up on the doorstep to profess his undying love. When she told him in no uncertain terms that she was not interested, he became furious. He chased her along the terraced garden and down to the stable block. She knew there was a piggery located next door and thought that she would be safe there. Alas, when Jane arrived at the door, it was locked. She then ran back up the hill, but George Bryce caught up with her beside the house and slit her neck with a cutthroat razor. The razor, which was used in evidence at the subsequent High Court trial on 30 May 1864, is today kept in an airtight polypropylene container. It has a steel blade and a wooden handle secured with brass pins, and can be seen at the Scottish Record Office, along with a plan of the footpath where the murder was committed.

Elizabeth returned to Ratho some years after her parents sold the house and met the new owners at a party. They told her that their son, who was the same age as she had been when she lived there, frequently complained of hearing footsteps during the night on the garden path outside the same bedroom window.

David Ingram, an antique dealer and past president of the Scottish Arts Club, who in addition operates an upmarket bed and breakfast establishment in Edinburgh's Georgian New Town, was summoned to value the contents of a small mansion near Dunfermline, right on the shores of the Firth of Forth. The house itself appeared to be eighteenth century, but it was obvious that certain parts of it dated from a much earlier period, which, however, had little relevance to the purpose of David's visit.

It was an all-day audit, and at one stage David announced to the owners that he needed to relieve himself and was directed down a passageway to a door on the right hand side. Faced with three doors, he opened the first one and was instantly aware of a darkened cellar, a black hole in the corner of which was a huddle of figures wearing monkish robes and obviously terrified at his intrusion. 'They began to give out tortured wailing sounds of sheer anguish,' says David who will never forget the experience. 'It was like a prolonged aaaaaagh! They clung to each other as if expecting to die.'

As one might imagine, David promptly

closed the door and retreated up the passageway, deciding not to tell the owners whom he concluded would clearly think he was mad. However, he did ask about the origins of the property and was told that long, long ago, at least 1,000 years previously, it had been the site of a monastery. David, who insists he is not normally susceptible to such flights of fancy, is convinced that he had a vision of monks hiding from some terrible invasion, possibly from Viking raiders who are known to have plundered regularly along this coast.

This is yet another example where monastic and religious figures predominate in the general run of supernatural imagery. Could it be that those in close proximity to higher powers have a greater hold than less spiritual figures on the mortal world?

When he was twelve years old, Jamie Walker, the young entrepreneur behind the Adelphi Distillery Company in Edinburgh, was putting the dogs out for a run at Newark Castle, his family home, by Ayr. It was a particularly gloomy evening, and through the mist he noticed a small gathering of black hooded men standing around what looked like a hanging tree some fifty yards from the side of the house. 'They were chanting something, but I couldn't make out the words,' he says. 'The dogs ran off in the opposite direction and according to my mother I ran back into the house as white as a sheet,' he says.

What makes this all the more significant is that Newark Castle once belonged to the enormously powerful Kennedy family who in the early sixteenth century became earls of Cassilis, and later marquesses of Ailsa. Ruthless and land hungry, the fourth Earl of Cassilis had his headquarters at nearby Dunure Castle, now a ruin, but from which, tradition has it, there is a secret underground passage connecting with Newark.

Now at the time of the Reformation, the Benedictine monks of Crossraguel Abbey, south of Maybole, in addition to the Abbey itself and a town house in Ayr, owned eight parishes and twenty-seven manors in the region. As the dominant political figure locally, with virtually limitless authority, the fourth Earl of Cassilis had long had his eye on the abbey lands, but had let matters rest since they were overseen by his kinsman Quintin Kennedy.

Quintin Kennedy, however, died in 1564, and six years later Cassilis summoned the unfortunate lay abbot, Allan Steuart, to Dunure for a chat. It was his earnest hope, he told him, that he, Steuart, might be persuaded to sign over the appropriate acres without a fuss. Not in the least bit impressed, the holy man politely declined, but when the Earl had him roasted over an open fire, succumbed and signed the necessary document. Thereafter, the Scottish Privy Council made a token protest, but that was that. The Kennedys prospered and went on to abandon Dunure and Newark and build the spectacular Culzean Castle as a showpiece for their wealth and success.

The monks of Crossraguel, which today stands ruined, were known as 'black monks' because they wore long black woollen robes with cowls. In all possibility, the gathering witnessed by Jamie Walker was a protest meeting being held by some of their number who, even now, are disinclined to let the matter rest in peace.

Twenty-six April 2002 saw the end of an era with the closing of BBC Scotland's Broadcasting House at 5, Queen Street. Since its beginning in the 1770s, this building or indeed buildings, since the complex eventually incorporated both 4 and 6, Queen Street, housed many different uses, at one time accommodating the Royal Philosophical Library and becoming at different stages a lecture theatre, where the great Victorian writer Charles Dickens spoke on a number of occasions, a hospital and a YMCA hostel before being acquired as the BBC's Edinburgh headquarters in October 1929.

Everyone who worked there over those years soon was made aware of its past and of the hauntings that took place in the rooms and corridors on an almost regular basis, mostly after the building had been full of people. Was this the reaction of the spirits within to the invasion from without? Nobody can know for sure, but over time the stories have accumulated.

And it was impossible to ignore them, especially if you were among those who stayed on in the building late at night. In particular if you found yourself in the passageway leading from the canteen, which had once been double the height, or rather depth, having been split into rooms on two floors. For over twenty years Lee Macphail worked in the building as a sound producer, and on more than one occasion saw the tall, translucent figure in the black cloak gliding past. As did his wife Debbie, also a producer.

'An old friend of mine,' says their veteran colleague John Gray who was first shown around the building in 1934 and joined the BBC staff full time in 1940. 'Everyone saw it sooner or later.'

Ellie Buchanan, writer, musician and broadcaster, who records songs under the name of Woodstock Taylor, was working there late in 1991, 'quite sober' she insists, when the Darth Vader look-alike passed her studio door. Convinced it was a prank, she rushed into the corridor to find nobody there. 'I was certain somebody was mobbing me up, but I never discovered whom,' she says.

It was only when the door handles began to rattle on another night and she knew for certain she was all alone in that particular part of the building, that she became concerned. 'I don't think I was frightened,' she insists. 'I just became annoyed because I thought somebody was making fun of me.'

Brian Morton, who hosts his own radio talk show, remembers an evening when his computer crashed and the lights turned on and off for no apparent reason. Head of Radio Drama Patrick Rayner was told about the sobbing sounds heard coming from the toilets in the basement area. Lee Macphail heard them too one night when returning tape recording equipment to his studio around 3 a.m.

John Gray is convinced that the spectre is a woman. 'One fantasy explanation is that she was a jilted lover of Dickens, who had a reputation with the ladies,' he says. 'She haunts the place because she got fed up with hearing the same old stories again and again.'

14

The Curse of the Drum

It fell upon a bonnie summer day,
When green grew oats and barley,
That there fell oot a great dispute
Between Argyle and Airlie.

'The Bonnie House o' Airlie',
(Ballad c. 1790, author unknown)

At Cortachy Castle, the Earl of Airlie's home at the end of Glen Clova in Angus, can be seen the remains of the Airlie Drum. As is so often the case when word is passed down through the generations, there is more than one variation on the story behind this. Some say that it belonged to a handsome young Clan Ogilvy drummer-boy who caught the eye of a long ago Countess of Airlie and was thrown from the battlements of nearby Airlie Castle by her jealous husband.

The more popular version, however, is that when Airlie Castle, the clan's main stronghold, came under attack from the eighth Earl of Argyll in 1641, a drummer-boy was despatched to deliver an ultimatum to the Royalist-supporting Ogilvys. They responded by taking the boy hostage and encasing him in his drum, which they suspended from a turret. The boy died still drumming on the inside of his instrument, but before doing so, uttered a curse that he would beat the drum whenever a member of the Airlie family was about to die.

The drum has certainly lived up to expectations, being heard prior to the death of two countesses in 1835 and 1845, and shortly before the death of the ninth Earl in 1849. Edinburgh businessman William Macnair recalls his grandmother Joan Newbigging telling him how her uncle had in June 1900 taken one of the lodges at Airlie. During the night, servants from the castle began to arrive asking to sleep at the lodge because they were being kept awake by the sound of drumming. Shortly afterwards it was announced that the eleventh Lord Airlie, who was in South Africa fighting in the Boer War, had been killed leading the 12th Lancers in a charge to save the guns at Diamond Hill, near Pretoria, in the Transvaal.

Marioth Hay adds a further slant to the mystery. In October 1917, Cortachy Castle was rented to some wealthy Americans who entertained lavishly. Marioth's uncle, Lord

Tweeddale, was in their house party and following a particularly riotous dinner, one of the guests produced the drum and marched around the house playing it, much to the amusement of those present. The following morning they heard the news that Patrick Ogilvy, the eleventh Earl's son, serving with the Irish Guards, had been killed in action.

It was in January 1958 that a group of National Service recruits, began their training with the Queen's Own Cameron Highlanders. They found themselves stationed at Fort George for a parade under the command of Major David Murray, who much later, as Colonel David Murray, was to revolutionize the quality of pipe music at the Edinburgh Military Tattoo.

Major Murray had the reputation of being a tough and demanding officer, and instead of being quartered in the barracks, he insisted that his soldiers slept out on the foreshore. 'The morning dip was a bit of a challenge,' recalls David Salkeld, who now lives in England and will never forget the experience. Following the parade, the men climbed Ben Nevis in heavy snow, wearing only their kilts and battledress tops, and afterwards set off to march through the Corryarick Pass, which divides Glenmore and Upper Strathspey, to Fort Augustus, starting off in the early morning. 'There were about thirty of us,' says Salkeld. 'It was snowing heavily and it took us most of the day. The going was incredibly tough and it was becoming dark when we suddenly heard the sound of bagpipes. It was such a relief because we thought that we must be getting close to our destination.'

The sound of pipes continued nearby, but it was not until some time later that the young men reached camp, totally exhausted, and immediately somebody mentioned the pipers. 'What pipers?' came the response.

There were no pipers either to be seen or heard in the camp. Indeed, so far as anybody knew there was nobody who played the pipes within a five mile radius.

'All of us heard the pipes that day, encouraging us to keep on going,' says Salkeld. 'But it was only afterwards that we realized that the tunes had been odd. They were all old fashioned variations on a theme. We all knew what we had heard, yet there was no explanation for it.'

A further incident involving the sound of bagpipes took place during the childhood of Shona Downie, who was brought up in the west end of Aberdeen in a house overlooking Allenvale Cemetery. It was New Year's Eve and she and her brother had been allowed to wait up for Old Bessie who lived nearby and was coming to first foot them. It was just after midnight, and they heard a knocking at the window. Rushing outside, there was nobody there.

After that they climbed to the top of the house which had a window overlooking the street. It was bitterly cold and snowing, and the knocking came again. Opening the window, they could still not see anybody, but they heard the sound of pipes coming from the graveyard, and what sounded like a party in full fling.

Every year thereafter, throughout her childhood, Shona and members of her family, immediately after the bells would hear bagpipe music and the sounds of a party coming from the graveyard. Yet there was never any mortal presence to be seen.

Another musical instrument associated with the Highlands of Scotland, and particularly with the great Clans of the North when they were still powerful, is the clarsach, the Gaelic harp. As recently as the 1970s it had almost disappeared until its music was revived by a group of enthusiasts.

South of Inverness, in the difficult days after the 1745 Jacobite uprising, lived two sisters, one of considerable beauty, the other talented but plain. During the conflict, their father, a widower who considered himself a-political, had avoided becoming involved in the fighting. He had little patience with either Prince Charles Edward Stuart or King George II, and had kept his family close to home, counting his blessing that he had no son. Mercifully, they had been left in peace, and in the evenings that followed the bloodbath of the Battle of Culloden, he took solace in listening to his younger daughter Morag playing the clarsach.

Contrary to first impression, the clarsach is a very different instrument from the harp in that its strings are played not with the fingers, but with the finger nails. The sound had a compelling resonance, and with the windows of the house open, in the still night air, the sound travelled. Even at a distance of two miles, the gentle music could be heard, rippling through the wooded landscape, and it soon attracted the attention of a young English soldier, stationed nearby in connection with the building of Fort George.

Intrigued, the young officer mounted his horse and followed the sounds, which brought him to the farm just as the music came to an end. When he knocked on the door, it was answered by one of the most ravishingly lovely girls he had ever set his eyes upon. Momentarily at a loss for words, he was on the brink of presenting his compliments when her father arrived behind her, and dismissed her inside. Thereupon, having taken stock of his uniform, the older man informed him that while he had no allegiance in the recent conflict, he was a pacifist, and strangers were not welcome.

For days and weeks thereafter, towards sunset, the soldier would ride over to the ridge overlooking the farm just to listen to the exquisite music, and one afternoon, having positioned himself early, he saw again the pretty girl of his first visit. And much to his dismay and pleasure, in equal measures, he encountered her coming up the path towards him carrying a basket which she promptly dropped, spilling the contents.

Whichever one of them was the more overcome with emotion, it was impossible to know, for she too had been dazzled by the good looks of the soldier. He learned that her name was Isla Mackinnon, and she learned that his was Captain Jones. He told her how much he admired her music, and she blushed, failing to admit that it was her younger sister Morag who was the musician.

Thereafter, whenever possible, they would meet. It was not difficult to do so. Her parents often sent her for messages, and he was good at inventing reasons for being out-and-about to his commanding officer. In the late afternoon, he would wait on the ridge to listen to her play the clarsach entirely unaware that it was someone else who did so.

Then came the summons for Captain Jones to join the forces of General Wolfe in Canada. The news was devastating for neither had fully appreciated the depth of their feelings for each other. Furthermore, Isla was convinced that her father would never agree to her going with him, let alone marrying him. She was, however, past the age of consent, so they decided to elope. They were young and reckless and in love.

But to run away from her family and everything she knew without telling anybody was unbearable, so on the eve of their departure, Isla confessed everything to her sister. Now Morag Mackinnon was a kindly soul, but prudish. She loved her sister and was horrified when Isla confided in her. She went at once to her father, who in a storm of righteous fury, confined Isla to her room so that she missed her assignation with Captain Jones. The Captain, assuming she had changed her mind, set off without her.

When he later wrote to her from Canada, there was no reply. Twenty-five years passed and now a full colonel with distinguished military honours, he found himself once again in Scotland and, travelling north of Perth, decided on a whim to make a detour to the farm he remembered so well. A man who had fought on the Plains of Abraham could not be said to lack courage, but he felt increasingly nervous as he grew closer to where the lovers had kept their tryst. Just as he was approaching, however, he saw a middle-aged woman on the pathway, and when she turned, the first thing he recognized was her eyes. They were Isla's eyes, but the face was round and tired, the body plump. The once golden hair, now grey, was tied back and tucked into a bonnet.

'Can I help you?' she asked without any sign of recognition.

He hesitated. 'I was looking for Miss Mackinnon,' he said.

She seemed surprised. 'Do I know you?' she asked.

'Captain Jones, Ma'am. You surely haven't forgotten?'

It took Morag Mackinnon less than a second to recognize the name and to identify the stranger. 'Why, of course,' she said calmly, and invited him to come with her to the farm. She was on her own now, she informed him, but her servant would serve refreshments. Her parent and older sister had passed on some time before, and she now ran the farm with the help of a manager.

It was also perfectly obvious to Morag that her visitor had mistaken her for Isla, and captivated by his manners and handsome head, she felt no desire to disillusion him. Before he departed that afternoon, she took up the clarsach and sang for him. He was visibly moved and, as he took his leave, asked if he might call again. 'We have already wasted so much time,' he said as he climbed into the saddle of his horse.

Morag was desperately unsettled. Ever since the betrayal, she had watched her sister Isla sink into the deepest melancholy. She had wished again and again that her mother could have been alive to tell them what to do. The Mackinnon father had not the slightest understanding of women, and had become impossible, forbidding either daughter her freedom. When invited to neighbouring farms, they were forced to stay at home. When gentlemen called, they were told to keep out of sight.

Although Morag never saw her sister smile again, Isla had never reproached her for what she had done. As her looks slowly faded, she turned increasingly to the Bible for solace. To all who knew her she behaved as a dutiful daughter to her father until at last she was taken by pneumonia at the age of thirty-seven. Heartbroken, but resolute in his faith and belief that he had acted as any parent would have done, her father followed Isla to the grave six months later.

After that Morag's guilt had known no bounds, but when the Colonel began calling upon her, she knew she could make him happy. There was no longer anybody to tell her what to do, and after years of subservience to her father's wishes, she felt she deserved some happiness. When the Colonel proposed to her, she accepted at once and they were married in Dunkeld. In the wedding vows, Morag took her sister's name of Isla.

The Colonel never knew that he had been deceived, and after they had dined he would often ask his wife to play her clarsach as she had done for him when they had first met and he had hidden on the ridge above the farm. And it was on one such occasion that two of the strings inexplicably broke. They were replaced, and almost at once two of the other strings snapped, then another. When this happened again, the Colonel's wife, overcome with remorse and a sense of being watched by her sister, fled upstairs to her dressing room and vowed that never again would she play the wretched instrument.

Much to the amazement of both the

Colonel and his wife, since they were both well over forty, they were blessed with a child, a girl, who was christened Morag. The child grew up to be a beauty, bearing an uncanny likeness to her aunt. The Colonel lived to see her happily married in turn, and shortly before her own death, Mrs Jones told her daughter the story of her life. From under a heavy canvas covering, she produced the clarsach with its broken strings and handed it over for safekeeping. The clarsach remains with her descendants to this day, and the strings have never been replaced.

The number of Scottish Regiments has been drastically reduced in the past two decades, but those that survive retain high standards of loyalty to the Crown and continue to play an important role in the safekeeping of our nation.

Army officer training teaches its recruits to be logical and decisive and to react fast in the best interests of resolving a situation. Soldiers are not easily taken in by illusion. Therefore, neither Brigadier Charles Ritchie, nor his brother officer Major David Dickson, is prone to flights of fancy. Both served with distinction with The Royal Scots, the 1st Regiment of Foot, which has its origins in antiquity and on occasion is referred to as 'Pontius Pilate's Bodyguard.'

The year was 1977, and Charles, then a major, and David, a captain, were stationed in a barracks building where they, and another officer, were allocated accommodation in the Mess. The other officers occupied quarters in an annexe.

'It was a weekday evening,' recalls Charles. 'I had gone to bed and was in a deep sleep when about midnight I was woken up by this terrible noise. My bedroom was on the first floor, and it sounded as if heavy furniture was being scraped across the wooden floor of the room below. I knew that nobody was supposed to be there, so I got out of bed, put on my dressing gown and went to investigate.'

At the end of the corridor he met up with David Dickson who had also been disturbed by the noise. 'By then the din was deafening with the sound of people shouting at one another, although what language they were talking in was quite indistinguishable. It was just a babble,' says Charles.

The barracks was an old stone building and as the two officers reached the bottom of the steps to the floor below, the sound came to an abrupt halt. The din had seemingly been coming from what was known as the Ladies' Room, a large chamber used for entertaining, and measuring approximately 16 feet by 49 feet. When the noise stopped Ritchie and

Dickson ran to the door and threw it open, but when they entered the room they saw immediately that it was empty. 'It was completely bare,' recalls Ritchie. 'There was not a stick of furniture in it. David and I just looked at each other, thinking what on earth was that all about?'

There was no intelligent explanation. The two of them split up and went around the Mess looking for intruders on the assumption that some of the soldiers might have been playing an elaborate hoax, but they found nobody. When they later mentioned it to the staff, they were told that yes, the building was known to be haunted. Weird things had happened before. On the subterranean floor there was a gymnasium, a chapel and an underground shooting range. Sometimes the night drinks trolley rattled violently for no apparent reason and Ritchie and some of the other officers even looked to see if a practical joker had attached it to a fishing line.

'Then there was another occasion when all of the room lights in the Mess dining-room suddenly clunked out,' says Ritchie. 'It happened when the Mess Corporal was laying out for a late dinner after a boxing match. All of the lights operated off a central switching post and he could actually see the switches clicking off as the bulbs went out, one after the other. But so far as he could tell, there was nobody physically doing it. It was quite extraordinary. None of us knew what to make of it.'

Pure fantasy is the most likely explanation, but while on the subject of soldiers and the British Army, there have been various reports over the centuries relating to the 9th Hispana Legion of the Roman Army. Despatched to Scotland by the Emperor Hadrianus in AD 117, they disappeared without trace. The historian Archie McKerracher writes that on a September night in 1974, when he was living on a housing estate on a hill above Dunblane, he heard a great noise that sounded like marching men. The sound became stronger as it drew nearer, and then passed immediately behind the houses on the other side of the street from his home. He thought he must have been overworking until some neighbours confirmed that they too had had heard the din.

McKerracher later discovered that his home was situated on the site of what had been a large Roman marching camp. An old Roman road ran directly behind the houses across the road from where he lived. But after two thousand years could this possibly have anything to do with what he heard that night? There are those who are convinced that it does.

The 9th Hispana Legion was quartered at York when the Caledonian tribes rose up in revolt and began attacking the Roman encampments that had been established as far north as Aberdeenshire. Sarah Dickson, a hotel receptionist, recalls a holiday in a remote cottage on a Perthshire estate and being woken up around 2 a.m. Glancing out of the window, she saw a procession of lights on the far side of the loch. 'There must have been at least fifty of them,' she says. 'There was a bright moon, but the lights were too far away for me to make out who or what was carrying them. They moved down the hillside and alongside the loch, and then disappeared into the distance. When I asked one of the estate workers what they were, he just laughed and told me that it was either poachers or the Lost Legion!'

Michael Scobie, a marine biologist and enthusiastic hill walker is more specific. He and his girl friend Hennie had pitched a tent on the banks of the River Tay near Meiklour in Perthshire. It had begun to rain, so they retired to their sleeping bags early. It was towards dawn that Hennie shook him awake and told him to listen.

'There was a great deal of clatter and banging going on outside, and when we looked through the tent flap, we could see at least a dozen or more men trying to ford the river. They were only about 40 feet away from us and were heaving away at some sort of cart loaded up with metal objects. They were quite small in stature, wearing helmets and what appeared to be short tunics. We could hear their voices, but couldn't understand a word. The noise went on for about twenty minutes and then they disappeared into the water. I walked over to see what had happened to them, but there was nobody in sight.'

The fact that these figures appeared to be wearing tunics does not necessarily signify that they were either soldiers on a field exercise or, indeed, Roman centurions.

What Michael and Hennie are convinced they saw could have been a group of college students on a holiday romp, a caravan of New Age travellers, members of some eccentric hiking or a hill-walking club, or even a film crew in the process of making some cinematic epic.

It is remarkably easy to make fun of such apparitions, but the question still remains unanswered. If none of these things, who or what on earth were they?

15

The Once and Future King

Then did their loss his foeman know;
Their King, their Lords, their mightiest
   low,
They melted from the field as snow,
When streams are swoln and south
   winds blow,
Dissolves in silent dew.

Sir Walter Scott, *Marmion*,
'The Battle' XXXIV

At some point in our lives, many of us have
clearly experienced the sensation of having
been somewhere before; in another time, in
another lifetime. Locations we have never
knowingly visited before become strangely
familiar. We know where the doors are, where
the passages lead to, and where the rooms are
located. In the French language they call it
'déjà vu', but that does not entirely
encompass the emotions that go with it.

Taking this a stage further, there are people
whom we meet for the first time and we feel

that we already know them. Long ago, in another existence, perhaps, there were shared experiences, encounters of one sort or another. And here they are, just like us, having arrived in the same way. Is it simply our genetic memory kicking in, or could there indeed be such a thing as reincarnation?

A.J. Stewart, author of two best-selling books during the late 1960s and 1970s, has had to accept that reincarnation is a reality, which she has tried long to avoid. As she has stated in her second volume of autobiography *Died 1513 — Born 1929* (later re-issued as *King's Memory*): 'Had I grown up in a culture which allowed the possibility that man has more lives than one, I should have been spared much suffering.'

Her earlier book *Falcon — The autobiography of His Grace James the 4 King of Scots* (Presented by A.J. Stewart) was the one she never wanted to write. As she says: 'Had I been born any other soldier who died on Branxton Moor — today called Flodden — and remembered my dying there, I could have written about it freely, a splendid novella or a treatise in the making!'

As she complains in *Died 1513*, 'Why do they all want to remember being kings and princesses; personally, I hate it because it is embarrassing; also I get blamed by almost every historian and soldier for the loss at Flodden.' As a result, she remembers herself not as an heroic king, but as 'Flodden James.'

Throughout most of her life, A.J. has hated the idea of reincarnation. She remembers saying in her adolescent years: 'If we have lived before, it must mean that we shall have to live *again*. An horrendous thought!'

A.J. was born into this world as Ada F. Kay. (She took her husband's name of Stewart when they married in 1957. They were divorced amicably eight years later.) As a little girl, only child of a schoolmaster, born atop the moors of rural Lancashire, there was no-one who could have imprinted upon her infant mind memories of a battlefield where she had died, in armour, beneath the bill-hooks of the enemy.

In her infancy, memories included ship-building, envoys arriving at court — and two slightly irregular memories of being presented by her (then) father to his lords in council. Then there was a brief recall of riding out as a boy clad in scarlet, wearing a gold shoulder chain, at the head of a small group of horsemen passing through a castle gate which, at the age of six, she identified from an LMS poster in a railway station as Stirling Castle. As to whom she had been, she had no idea in those early days except that her homeland and place of duty was Scotland.

She was posted there for the first time as a private in the ATS in 1947. As soon as the night train from King's Cross Station reached Berwick in the grey light of dawn, she recalls recognizing the landscape from the carriage windows — the River Tweed, the Bass Rock and Edinburgh Castle. 'My heart filled with a gigantic gladness to be *home*,' she wrote.

Later, travelling to join her unit at Fairmilehead, she experienced a similar sensation.

At a certain point in the journey two strange things happened simultaneously. I had the sense that I had just received a tumultuous welcome, as though sur-rounded by an unseen cheering crowd and I realized that I knew the way. It was not the streets I recognized, but the landmarks. Trees and grass to my left with Arthur's Seat in the distance, to my right, I knew, there should be open water — and there it was, just a glimpse down a street all lined with houses. It was, I knew, the Forth, but I was puzzled by my own feeling that I should at that moment have seen a great deal more of it. I asked was the green expanse to my left a park? — receiving the reply that it was

'Bruntsfield Links'. The name to me sounded foreign, as though I had expected something else.'

With the realization that somehow she had been there before, came the search for an identity. 'My new life never fitted me; it was always like a glove cut and sewn to fit another hand,' she observed later.

When she returned to England, she pursued a career as a successful playwright. Its beginning was in Lancashire where her play based upon family anecdotes and local archives, finally made its mark in repertory theatre. Set between 1860 and 1864, its subject was the resistance of Lancashire to its plight during the Cotton Famine being used as an excuse for breaking the blockade against the southern states of America.

Warp and Weft played to full houses throughout Lancashire and became known as 'The Guild Play' when it was presented during Preston Guild Week to illustrate the 'craft' of the theatre. Rave notices abounded, but the response from London's West End management and agencies was 'a magnificent play, but its northern regional accent would not be understood down here by West End audiences.'

This made A.J. so angry that she set off to

London with a small suitcase, a small amount of cash, one telephone number of a friend, and there, in a toe-hold bedsitting-room, she wrote her best-known radio and stage work *The Man from Thermopylae*. It went on to become successful around the world while she was — still — escaping Scotland.

In the meantime, *Warp and Weft* under the new title *Red Rose for Ransom*, won a radio play competition and she was invited to join the central Script Section of BBC Television. In the years that followed, A.J. achieved status, a good income, and a more-or-less successful marriage, but it was not to last. 'Home to Scotland has been the dedication of all my days,' she says. Driven northwards, as ever, she headed home for Scotland in — again — a train from King's Cross Station.

Beginning in a bedsitting-room in Edinburgh, she continued to work for the BBC, and indulged in her own private writing. By this time the money was running out, as was also her creative connection with what she terms 'a world south of Watford.'

In Scotland, she keenly felt her lack of background knowledge. She asked her Gaelic tutor for recommended reading and miraculously he sent her *The Kingdom of Scotland* by Agnes Mure Mackenzie. A.J. had grown up in England where no Scottish history was ever taught. Thus for the first time in her life she met a Scot who lived 500 years ago. He was James IV, King of Scots, and she knew why he thought as he did.

While A.J. admired Agnes Mure Mackenzie's appreciation of James's intentions, she was surprised to find that so eminent and sensitive an historian had failed to grasp that James's 'Highland Policy' was part of a three-stage programme, interrupted by his death, and that the building of *The Great Michael*, the world's greatest warship of its time, had been for a deadly strategic purpose unseen by the historian. Mure Mackenzie's chapter ends at Flodden. It was a name that had haunted A.J. all of her life for no obvious reason and here, at last, she found the cipher of the James Stewart who died there. He was the fourth of that dynasty, IV being all too easily confused with VI in Roman numeracy.

It was a colossal national disaster, from whose consequences Scotland has never yet recovered. It is an eternal warning of the need for peaceful men to pay heed to armament. But there was a cause for neither shame nor rancour. It was fairly won and grievously lost. Only one man was dishonoured by it — Henry, who refused the mere decency of burial of his sister's husband, killed in fair battle. James was given no grave: no man knows where he lies today. His people refused to believe he was dead, though his body in fact was found and borne to Henry. They said he had but gone to Jerusalem and would ride home once more to be their friend and leader: but the years passed, and he never came again.

It was the paragraph's ending '*he never came again*' which shocked her the most. She found herself crying out, 'It's not true! It's not true!'

During the next four years a great culmination of coincidences began to take place. A.J.'s determination to see Scotland as a separate place from Watford and Westminster resulted in the rejection of almost every script she wrote. The last to appear on television was *Hills Beyond the Smoke* written in collaboration with her old colleague of BBC years, the late Alistair Bell, who was being posted back to London because the studios in Glasgow were being turned over to 'English classics'.

The production, directed by Pharic Maclaren, was the nearest she could get to a statement of independence. It was a dead time for Scottish playwrights, and A.J. was the first to speak out on the subject openly. To little effect. A pilot script, *The Common Stair*, which she believed could have become a serious statement about life in Scotland, died against the wall.

Meanwhile, *The Man from Thermopolae* marched from strength to strength. The radio play had travelled the world, from Australia to Radio Free Czecholovakia, from Germany to South Africa, anywhere that the human soul determined its own end. Even in Scotland it had a place when the Gateway Theatre in Edinburgh produced A.J.'s first stage version in 1961, and it was later produced in 1965 as part of the official Edinburgh Festival programme.

'Everyone wanted *The Man from Thermopolae*, a play about human life in ancient Sparta, but there was still no place for human life in Scotland,' she says. 'This is what we set out to achieve with the Society of Scottish Playwrights which I helped to start up but which sadly no longer exists.'

At last, defeated by humdrum reality, she reached for her typewriter and a voice from another century called out.

Why did she find it so impossible to read what others had written about James IV? Why did she have so much information in her head about him apparently unknown to historians?

How was she able to think with his voice on her typewriter?

'The sentences used to come like a driving wind at the back of my skull,' she says. Her play was later commissioned by the late Iain Cuthbertson for production in Perth on the recommendation of the Scottish patriot Wendy Wood.

Then one day she came across the portrait of James by Jacques le Boucq which features on the front cover of R.L. Mackie's biography of the king. Instead of noticing the extraordinary resemblance it bore to herself, she found herself saying out loud, 'I do wish he had paid more attention when I told him about drawing my thumb from the *wrist* . . . '

She was later to learn that le Boucq's portrait is known as 'the portrait with the unfinished hands.'

A.J.'s discovery of her alter ego was to be a long and painful process, not least because from the very start it never crossed her mind that in a previous existence she could have been a man.

Essentially feminine, this revelation understandably undermined her completely. The realization began with a dressing gown of patchwork she had designed and made during the austerity period at the end of the war. Decorated with appliquéd fleur de lys, its mediaeval character had been a joke to her until in 1965 she became conscious of its presence hanging behind her bedroom door.

During the summer sales, in Tollcross, she picked up a pair of thick black tights, at that time still an innovation. To these was added a long black polo-necked tunic which she belted first with gold kid to match gold shoes for a party. Later, finding herself doing so much at home in this outfit, she changed the gold shoes to black and wore it on the day her BBC script editor James Brabazon came up to visit her from London.

'You look like a cadet from an elite cavalry school,' he told her, and they both laughed.

However, by this time she was finding it increasingly difficult to wear skirts, except for long ones during the evening. She sent off to Leff and Jason, the London-based theatrical costumiers, for more heavy black nylon practice tights and she searched the shops for matching tunics. This was now her daily wear which passed almost unnoticed because of the arrival of the mini-skirt.

To her great amusement, she came across a cartoon in the *Edinburgh Evening News* of pedestrians on Princes Street showing all the women dressed up like mediaeval pages and the hippy men trailing along in gowns. 'At least fashion has been kind to me,' she reflects. 'Imagine what it would have been like had my earlier life been that of Mr Gladstone . . . '

For twelve months after A.J. finished writing *Falcon*, it felt as if she was wearing a plastic membrane separating her from the world around her.

'It took me up to twenty years to get out of wearing black tights and a tunic,' she says. But dressing for the part helped her to come to terms with herself. 'I think that if a lot of people who become transvestites or transsexuals were able to recognize that in a previous life they might have been of a different gender and a different historic style, it might enable them to unravel their problems. There are an awful lot of obscure half-and-half conditions that people simply do not understand.'

A.J. finally faced reality while staying with a friend in Jedburgh the night before she at long last returned to Flodden battlefield. It was he who came rushing to her room at the sound of her screams and helped her to confront her fears.

'So you are James IV?' he asked her in a matter of fact tone. He had had a similar precognitive experience in Greece and as he patiently re-assured her, she noticed that the steel shutter within her head was suddenly gone.

In the morning, she confronted her worst fears by visiting the battlefield where she found absolution. Turning to walk slowly back down the hill, she felt suddenly light-hearted and liberated. Having opened the wicker gate at the end of the footpath, she stepped through into the twentieth century. As she says:

Writing *Falcon* completely destroyed my life. My obsession about getting myself back to Scotland wrecked my marriage and ended my career as a playwright. I always thought that once I had got it all out of my system I could return to normal, but nobody would let me. I had originally intended for *Falcon* to be published anonymously, but then I discovered that copyright can not be assigned to a defunct king! So it became *Falcon — The Autobiography of His Grace James the 4 King of Scots*, (Presented by A. J. Stewart).

And now she has a third book to write, because everybody wants to know what happened next. Unfortunately, it is not as simple as that.

In *Died 1513 — Born 1929*, she records:

There was now a new person working at my typewriter whose ghost-hands no longer required the subterfuge of scribbling cryptic messages disguised as verse: there was no nocturnal poetry written during the period. He works overtly now, channelling our life's single passion into letters and play scripts. I still watched my hands with curiosity, but their antiquity worried me no more. As long as they flew across the keys to convey our meaning, I did not care whose hands they were — and had been.

A.J. knows that to write her next book she must once again confront her demons. Since the age of three she has had dreams about sixteenth-century court life, but she dreams them as James.

Neither he nor A.J. appear in these dreams. They are about what takes place around them.

During the writing of *Falcon*, A.J. avoided all the places of her James-time because she wished to see them as they remained in her memory. Craigmillar she had visited by accident and it bore little resemblance to the cosy place she had known. There were walls where there should not have been walls. 'All these damned modern renovations!' she had stormed as she led her accidentally assembled party around the building during the Craigmillar Festival.

In the case of Linlithgow, which she still pronounces 'Li'lithgow', she has described it from memory in *Falcon* in 1488 when she arrived there with the rebels, and she later described her own 'modern renovations'.

When the book was published, she made an excursion to the Palace accompanied by her cousin John, a chartered surveyor, and to her annoyance, found that the original entrance of 1488 had been sealed off.

'I then made a tour,' she says. 'What I wanted to know was had they cured that awful smell of stale food which, in 1488, used to wend its way up the stair to the hall from the old kitchens. When I had the Palace renovated, I had that stair removed, so it is just a turret now. I recognized it and marched John smartly across to it. It was, in fact, the back view of the then closed old entrance. As soon as we got there, I said to John, 'No! No! You can still smell the trace of the old dinners!'

'Well, I could, but John, as a surveyor, was more interested in the walls above me. 'Yes,' he said. 'There are the ends of the treads which remained after you removed the staircase.' '

On another occasion she agreed to take part in a documentary film for the television programme *Nationwide*. 'They filmed me on the roof walk at Lil'ithgow, which used to be my favourite when I was King, but I refused to wear a microphone saying to them I'd record my thoughts later at home. When I got back and they began to record me, the drawing room clock struck 4 p.m. My friends who saw the programme all told me afterwards that they loved the way that St Michael's had sounded the hour!'

Towards the completion of her second autobiography, A.J. became involved with a family who lived at Craigmillar. It was a large family with all of the social problems associated with being tenants on a soulless housing estate, but they used to visit her and she, in turn, called on them. Before long, she became friends with them and began to hear stories about a black horse.

Now while the court had been in residence at Falkland or Stirling, James used to ride his favourite black stallion from his bachelor establishment at Craigmillar to inspect the progress on *The Great Michael* in his shipyards at New Haven. When both horse and rider failed to return after Flodden, the rumours spread like a tidal wave. For almost nine decades, right up until Union of the Crowns in 1603, there were sightings of the black horse with its gold and scarlet harness. It had been a golden age and the people of Scotland liked to remember the good times.

After 1603, the story was forgotten, that is until the late 1920s when reports of a great black stallion at the gates of Craigmillar Castle began to circulate again. Although it is unusual to find anybody in Craigmillar who will actually admit to having seen the stallion, most know somebody else who has. And surely it cannot be pure coincidence that the legend should have re-emerged around about the same time that Ada F. Kay was born?

A.J. has started her next book, but finds the process of writing no less painful than it was previously. 'From my own experience and from the letters I have received from readers, it is obvious that there are many more people who remember their own previous lives than are willing to admit it,' she says.

Those letters which I have welcomed and acknowledged, usually come from people who have died violently, as I did. Most are soldiers and sailors, of many ranks and incidentally, also a burned 'witch' whose graphic description of her last moments is something which I, a professional writer, could never have imagined.

Are you surprised if those of us who died violently remember it? The last memory one has of life is of hatred. It is personal. I was aged forty, in the vigour of manhood, being hacked down by five billhooks. The sight of those blades beyond my vizor is with me yet. When the memory came back to me, I even dashed off a drawing of those blades beyond my vizor grill. History tells me that it was an arrow to the throat that laid me low, and for years I have denied it — there was no arrow, I said. I swore it was a blow on the head — but . . . I may have been wrong in that. Something temporarily rendered me unconscious, lying on my back. 'Seeing stars' is the usual description of what took place. Remembering the clout to the back of my head may possibly be just the memory of my hitting the ground. I doubt whether many people who die in battle, adrenaline cutting out the pain, have time for a forensic diagnosis of their injuries before the *coup de grâce*. Certainly I had none.

Despite the restoration of a Scottish parliament in 1999, there is still another length to go for A.J. Nothing less than full independence. Thirty years ago she promised doubting voters on their doorsteps that it would happen again in *this* lifetime. That, she said, was the reason she was here. A tall claim? Not really, so far as she is concerned.

A.J. is an a-political animal who sees small difference between modern political parties and the court factions which made life trying in the fifteenth and sixteenth centuries. She has mixed feelings about the Scottish parliament, but they are passionate.

'They are learners and beginners, but they need soon to learn what state craft is about,' she says.

As James Stewart, King at fifteen — and never a minor — he/she too had to learn fast. There is no place for ego and lusting after power; there is no place for factions and self-serving publicity. 'There is no place for civil war in a nation struggling to regain its sovereignty after centuries of divide-and-rule, at which 'King England' has always been adept,' she says.

However, A.J. herself wants no part in either parliament or politics. She has worked in her own way to make Scotland visible. 'I have done my stint on television, radio and film to remind the world that Scotland has an historic past of world distinction long before it became boxed and shortbread tinned as Charles Edward or ruffed and capped as Mary,' she says.

A.J. admits that she is now rather tired of it all. 'My job is simply to help sustain the energy of Scotland which keeps forever fighting that battle which I lost. I have no other role.'

Her hopes for the future? 'A free Scotland; a sovereign Scotland — and just myself safely dead and buried with another five hundred year holiday ahead. No, make it a thousand, off-duty!'

16

A Giant in the Woods

And such a phantom, too, 'tis said,
With Highland broadsword, targe, and
 plaid,
And fingers red with gore,
Is seen in Rothiemurchus glade . . .

Sir Walter Scott, *Marmion*,
'The Camp' XXII

In a secluded corner of the Forest of Rothiemurchus estate is the burial place of Seath Mor Sgor Fhiaclach, a chief of the Clan Shaw who lived in the late fourteenth century. Shaw was by reputation a formidable warrior, standing over six feet tall with a twisted smile that struck terror into the hearts of even his own followers. Travellers through the woods, passing through a wooded glade, have spoken of encounters with a gigantic figure challenging them to battle. If they accept, no harm is done, but should they show fear they are never seen again.

In *Memoirs of a Highland Lady*, Elizabeth

Grant of Rothiemurchus writes of the troublesome Shaws. During the sixteenth century, when a Shaw chief was killed in a fight, his body was taken to the kirkyard, but the following day materialized outside his widow's door at Dalnavert. It was buried again, and again it was raised, and this pattern continued until Laird James of Rothiemurchus announced he was tired of the game. He had the corpse buried deep down within the kirk beneath his own seat, and every Sunday when he went to pray, he stamped his feet upon the heavy stones he had laid over the remains of his enemy.

Although recent reports have confused this individual with Seath Mor, this is obviously not the same Shaw chief. Allegedly Seath Mor lived two centuries earlier, and his tomb lies outwith the kirk at a distance of twenty yards. However, placed on top of it are five cylindrical stones that resemble white cheeses. According to local legend, anyone who dares tamper with them will suffer the terrible revenge of the guardian spirit, an elf called Bodach an Duin (Goblin of the Doune). At the beginning of the nineteenth century, a footman in the service of the Duchess of Bedford, who had the lease of the Doune of Rothiemurchus, apparently decided to test the legend by throwing the centre stone of the five into the nearby River Spey. Three days later his body was recovered from the river and the stone was inexplicably in place again.

In 1984, Leslie Walker and two locals were in the process of restoring the graveyard when a party of visitors appeared asking to see the clan chief's tomb. Without giving it a second thought, Leslie and one of his colleagues, walked over to the plot to indicate the stones.

'At lunchtime I began to shiver violently and sweat was running off me like rain,' he is quoted as saying at the time.

When taken to hospital, his temperature had reached 103 degrees. He was kept there for three weeks and lost more than three stone in weight. He was fortunate. His friend suffered a cerebral haemorrhage.

Coincidence or not, five years later, in 1989, all of the stones disappeared from the remote churchyard. The loss was reported by Hazel Smith from Aviemore. 'Outsiders may think we are being foolish, but many people here believe the curse to be true,' she said in a newspaper interview at the time. Obviously, since it did not take long for the stones to be returned.

The circumstances surrounding more recent disappearances of the stones remain a puzzle, but evidence suggests that their removal had become something of a 'rite of passage' test for local youths. To make sure they remain in place in future, a wrought iron cover has since been erected to cover them.

Hidden in the woodland, a mile or so from Doune of Rothiemurchus, the ruined chapel and its immediate surroundings today give the appearance of being well cared for, albeit the handful of silver coins scattered across the surface of Seath Mor's plot adds a sinister dimension. Another occupant of the cemetery since 1971 is Lord Reith, the formidable first director-general of the BBC, whose favourite recreation was to walk to the top of nearby Cairngorm, 'to be closer to God', he said. Neither of these giants, one reflects, were men to be trifled with.

There are among us those who are particularly susceptible to the mood of a location, to places where a deed of great sadness has taken place, which suggests, of course, that the containment of a great evil lingers on long after it is first perpetrated.

Alanna Knight and her husband Alasdair once took two Australian visitors on a day trip to Inverness, diverting en route to the battlefield of Culloden Moor. 'I had never been there before, but since my mother was a MacDonald, I felt that it was about time that I did,' she said.

Over eight hundred Clanranald, Glencoe, Glengarry and Keppoch clansmen of Clan Donald fought for Bonnie Prince Charlie at Culloden, many of them butchered in the aftermath, and shortly after Alanna's arrival there, she began to feel dreadfully ill. 'I had this extraordinary headache and it was as if I was tasting blood,' she recalled. I told Alasdair he would have to look after Pat and Wayne, our Australian friends, while I went back to sit in the car park feeling nauseous. I had never felt so sick before in my life, and when they eventually returned to the car I was thinking that I might have to go to hospital. Then as soon as we drove off, my head cleared.'

Ten years later Alasdair and Alanna returned to Culloden, on this occasion with their sons Chris and Kevin, and exactly the same thing happened. 'My head was splitting and this time I decided to stay in the car,' said Alanna. 'Then as soon as the boys had had a look around and we set off again, the headache disappeared. It was extraordinary.'

Wendy Wood, the Scottish patriot who died in 1981, recorded an equally unsettling experience in her 1970 memoirs *Yours Sincerely For Scotland*. On her first visit to Culloden with a group of friends she had

213

leant over the Well of the Dead, where the dying and wounded from the battlefield had gathered for their last drink.

On that occasion, as I bent my head to look down into it, I saw not my own face, but that of a man. It was not reflection or distortion, for he had a starved face, huge eyes and long black hair. It quite unnecessarily terrified me, and I went scurrying back to my friends.

Anxious to convince herself that she had been imagining things, Wendy returned to the well years later to re-live the experience.

I bent over — the water was even further down, but there was the same man's face, his eyes staring into mine with agony, a cut right across the brow almost across his left eye, gaping raw flesh and blood running down, clotting the long black hair. The pain in my own brow was terrible, the staring, horror-stricken eyes seemed to be inside my own eyes. It is impossible in any medium to express how this terrifying person infiltrated my being, from a fusing, an amalgamation, to a knowledge of being one and the same person. I tore myself away, to realize that I was sobbing and hardly knew what I was doing.

Afterwards she recalls that she found herself unable to stop shaking. The pain over her left eye remained for nearly a week.

North of Inverness is an old farm near Dingwall where a baby was born to a recently married couple. It is not unusual for mothers to have periods of depression following a birth, but pretty soon afterwards Chrissie Douglas began seeing a small white cloud hanging over her bairn's cot. It unsettled her greatly, and one afternoon, returning inside from the garden where she had been hanging some washing, she saw the cloud hovering right over her baby's face. In desperation, she hurled the empty basket at the apparition. In that instant, the cloud moved and rushed towards her, up her out-flung arm, and then disappeared over her shoulder.

Chrissie felt a searing pain in her arm, and when she pulled back the sleeve of her blouse, there were four parallel burn marks running the length of her arm.

The doctor, when called to treat the burn, was baffled and in his concern for the mental health of the mother, related the story to the local landowner, Patrick Munro of Foulis, who agreed to consult their friend, the parish minister, the Revd Charles Robertson, now of Canongate Kirk in Edinburgh. When Robertson called on Chrissie, he told her that he was not sure what he could do to help her, but he would at least take steps to protect her baby.

He then asked if there had been any similar or unusual past-history associated with the farm, and it emerged that in the last century a child had been born out-of-wedlock to a couple who worked at the farm. To hide the shame of it, the father had insisted the baby be killed at birth, and the body hidden under the farmhouse doorstep. Inevitably, in a small country community, the truth eventually came out, and the couple were arrested, tried by the Sheriff of Dingwall and found guilty of murder.

Robertson next asked if any of the more recent tenants of the farm had had any untoward experiences relating to children. He was told that a previous tractor man on the farm and tenant of the farmhouse, now living in a neighbouring village, had once reported an odd occurrence. He and his wife had no family, but every Saturday his wife's sister and her husband came to spend the day with them, bringing their baby daughter with them. On this particular Saturday, the tractor man had come in from the fields at noon and, as usually, before the midday meal, had made for the bathroom upstairs to wash. As he reached the bottom of the very steep staircase, he looked up and saw his niece standing teetering on the top step. She had just learned to stand and was still uncertain on her feet. He thought to himself: 'Jean and the bairn must have come early. I mustn't startle the baby by calling on her. She might tumble down. I'll just creep up and gather her up.'

He walked very slowly and silently up the stairs, but when he reached the top there was no one there. Much to his amazement, the child seemed simply to have vanished, though he was absolutely certain she had been there.

Later in the afternoon, the visiting family arrived at their usual time, but they could offer no explanation as to what had happened. Robertson visited the by now retired tractor man and heard the story at first hand. He then knew what he must do.

He sensed that the poor, murdered bairn was simply homeless, cruelly deprived of her body at birth, and disposed of without being commended to God. She needed either a body to live out of and complete her life — and it seemed that the body of any baby girl who came into her presence would do — or she needed to be sent back home to God from whom she came.

Robertson now suggested that the child be

given an address to go to which, through a simple prayer service of commendation and blessing, he was happily able to provide. There were no further incidents at the farmhouse.

Exorcism, however, can be a dangerous business. Researching the life of James Thomson, composer of *The Seasons* and *Rule Britannia*, Borders-based literary critic Stuart B. Kelly recalls coming across a curious story concerning the demise of the poet's father. Born at Ednam in 1700, James was the third son and fourth child of Thomas Thomson, the minister of that place. Although Kelly is uncertain of the provenance of this story, it was certainly when the Thomson family had moved up Hobkirk way, south-east of Hawick. What Kelly remembers is that the Revd Thomas was called upon to perform an exorcism at a local farm when a kind of 'ignis fatuus' enveloped him.

'It took three days for him to die,' says Kelly. 'I was interested in it since Thomson junior was such an enlightenment man, and to have such rank superstition in the family must have had a significant impact on his psyche.'

Another example of where an exorcism went violently wrong involving fire took place in Fife some twenty years ago, at a location I have been requested not to divulge since some of the survivors, and one in particular, are still alive. It had started off as a light-hearted business, an attempt by some amateurs to try and put right a situation that had been bothering them for some time. If there is anything to be learned from the outcome, it is that amateurs should never play with fire.

At the centre of the plot was Joss Asher, a history graduate from St Andrews University who was renting a room in a large country mansion where the absentee owner was only too delighted to earn some extra cash from a family estate that was rapidly steering him into bankruptcy. Joss was one of seven students who during the university term made use of a wing of the old place. They shared a kitchen, a common sitting room and a dining room, and employed a cleaner to come in and give the rooms a good going over once a week. To have seen the state of it, you would never have realized this, but then students, especially students from well-heeled backgrounds, are not famous for their sense of tidiness or order. With almost monotonous regularity Mrs Cruikshank, their cleaner, who also 'did' for the rest of the house, would threaten to hand in her notice if their ways did not improve. Everybody knew, and if not she would remind them, that she and her mother before her had worked there for as long as anybody could remember, so nobody took her seriously.

Be that as it may, when Joss Asher graduated, he decided to stay on at the house to finish off a postgraduate degree, and by this time his girl friend Cheryl had moved in with him. It was Cheryl who first encountered the crazed figure on the staircase.

To set the scene, this was a rambling Victorian palace built on a site of far greater antiquity from the combined proceeds of the linoleum, flour, and jute industries. The family had done well for themselves, not least from military and naval careers, and the wood-panelled walls were covered with oil paintings of their ancestors.

Joss, who was pretentious for such credentials, felt comfortable in these surroundings. He even implied to those who might be interested that he was a relative. However, there was one particular portrait among the many on the staircase he found inexplicably unsettling. It was the likeness of a strong-jawed man with dark, piercing eyes penetrating deep into him every time he passed. An inscription on the over-size gold frame informed him that this gentleman's name was Captain Walker Duncan, RN.

Captain Duncan had been painted around the year 1797. Joss asked Mrs Cruikshank if she knew anything about him, and she gave him a sideways look. 'Bit of a bad lot, that one,' she said. 'Not really one of the family, but always claimed to be.'

At the time, Joss ignored the inference, thinking she was having a go at him. He was preoccupied with a dissertation and had been up all night working on it. It was the same night that Cheryl came dashing into the room to tell him that there was a burglar downstairs. Reluctantly he followed her to where she claimed to have seen the intruder, but if there had been anybody there to begin with, there was no longer anybody there.

'Did you get a good look at him?' asked Joss.

Looking over his shoulder, Cheryl pointed. 'He was the spitting image of that guy there.'

Without turning, Joss knew that she was pointing at the painting of Captain Walker Duncan, RN.

'Don't be ridiculous,' he snapped, at which she burst into tears.

The semester passed quickly that year, and it was after a rollicking celebration in early May that Joss returned to the house with Cheryl around dawn. As they pulled open the substantial oak door to let themselves into the doorway, they were suddenly confronted by a huge, angry spectre swathed in a black cloak. Open mouthed, all they could bring themselves to do was stand and stare at him as he rushed violently towards them, then vanished into thin air.

'My God, what was that?' exclaimed Joss, as Cheryl clung to him in fright.

Now Joss Asher possessed an intelligent mind and was not prone to hallucinations. Besides, Cheryl had been with him. On the following morning his first port of call was the library in St Andrews where he immersed himself in local records, with particular reference to the old families of the neighbourhood. It took him two days to track down the dirt on Captain Walker Duncan, RN, and even then it was only a footnote in some old transactions.

Walker Duncan was indeed the natural son of a former laird who had acknowledged him and brought him up, although being a bastard he was passed over for his younger brother who had been born in wedlock to another mother. Sent to sea on his sixteenth birthday, the lad distinguished himself in action against the Dutch fleet and became something of a local hero. When his father died and he inherited nothing, however, the resentment welled up inside of him and he swore that no matter how long it took him, he would have what was his by right.

Since the spoils of his naval career had made him financially self-supporting, what he presumably meant by 'his right' was, in fact, the house. It was perhaps fortunate for his siblings that shortly afterwards he was thrown from his horse riding cross country and broke his back. Nobody knows quite when his ghost took up residence in the house, but it was when his great-great-nephew, flush with marital wealth, doubled the size of the front façade and erected two turreted side pavilions that the presence of Captain Walker Duncan began to be noted on the staircase of the west wing.

There was only one course of action, announced Joss to his fellow lodgers — an exorcism. He had acquired a book on the subject and the sooner they set about it, the better.

To begin with it was treated as a bit of a joke, and some of the others thought it was a good excuse to have a party. Cases of wine and beer were provided. A séance was timed for midnight, and some of the girls turned up with boxes of candles and night lights to decorate the hallway.

It turned out to be an extraordinary evening, not helped by those present indulging in heavy drinking before anything got started. By the time everyone was assembled in a circle around Joss, who was holding an open bible, those who were not drunk were high spirited on something else.

As instructed, they all held hands and after a long pause, Joss began to recite the Lord's Prayer. Nobody can quite recall what then took place, but those who did give evidence afterwards spoke of a hurricane, a ball of fire, and an electrifying explosion. It took a good half hour for the fire engines to arrive, and by the time they did, the west wing had been gutted. Although everybody who had been at the party escaped with minor burns, none of the contents of the west wing were saved except for one of the paintings which the following morning mysteriously appeared on the gravel sweep outside. You might have guessed. It was the portrait of Captain Duncan.

In the police enquiry that followed, Joss was exonerated and the fire attributed to an electrical fault. All of the wall plugs throughout the building had been five amp with two pin sockets. Health and safety would nowadays never allow such an antiquated system in a commercially leased property. Nobody, other than the insurance company and the landlord, knows the full extent of the damage, but soon afterwards the estate was sold. After a great deal of demolition work and the introduction of a golf course, it is today owned by a multi-national leisure corporation and operated as a top holiday resort. It is interesting to note that the portrait of Captain Walker Duncan RN, identified as 'a former owner of the estate', takes pride of place in the lavishly refurbished hallway.

17

Second Sight

Oh Drumossie, thy bleak moor shall, ere many generations have passed, be stained with the best blood of the Highlands. Glad I am that I will not see that day, for it will be a fearful time.

Coinneach Odhar

The northern east and west coasts of Scotland abound in prophecy and legend. They say that those who work close to the soil see clearer, and in more detail, what is truly important in life. Nowhere is this more evident than in the everyday struggle of the crofter whose livelihood is achieved through pitting his strength and wits against whatever the elements throw at him.

Confronting nature in the raw, exposed to all the whims of the almighty, it comes as no surprise to discover those, tucked away among the remoter hills and glens, born with remarkable degrees of second sight.

In 1980, I was staying the weekend with

the late Jane Durham at Scotsburn, in Easter Ross, and Jane's niece, Sue Paterson, suggested we visit Swein MacDonald, the self-styled Highland Seer, in his croft on the slopes of the Struie at Ardgay, near Bonar Bridge. Now I had studied the prophecies of the seventeenth century Isle of Lewis-born Kenneth of Kintail, also known as Coinneach Odhar or the Brahan Seer, but the idea of a modern-day visionary holding court in the far north-east of Scotland left me highly sceptical.

It has to be said, however, that Kenneth of Kintail's predictions concerning the Highlands, despite three centuries of embellishment, are startlingly thought provoking. Could he really have foreseen the Highland Clearances, the advent of railways and bridges, the Dounreay Nuclear Reactor, and North Sea oil? Certainly, his forecast of the doom of the Mackenzies of Seaforth who were responsible for his being burned in a barrel of tar on Chanonry Point, makes chilling reading.

I could not help wondering how Swein MacDonald would rate in comparison, but then that says a lot about my own state of unbelief at the time. I was to be genuinely surprised.

To begin with Swein looked every bit the

part. A big bear of a chap, his face was weather-beaten, his eyes a clear shade of blue. Greying hair hung down to his shoulders, and his straggly beard, also grey, was full. Some years before he had been involved in an industrial accident and as a result, he walked with a stick. Another consequence was that he had lost all sense of taste and smell, but gained instead a form of tunnel vision which flashed up images of the future and the past, 'like in a film.'

Swein's family has crofted twenty acres at Kincardine Hill for over five hundred years. Swein was born in Elgin in 1931, went to the local school and worked as a stonemason before a stint in Glasgow employed by the Clyde Navigation Trust. He maintains, however, that he has always had second sight, inherited from his grandfather John, whose presence he often senses about the croft. He describes it as an inner vision, a third eye, very different from telepathy and mind-reading.

Given cups of coffee in the front room by his then wife Isabelle, we were each summoned to his 'consulting room' in turn for what he called a 'reading'. It was growing dark outside, and sticks of incense burned from a pot placed in front of the fireplace. He handed me a notebook and a pencil, and told me to take notes if I wanted to. Then he began. First he told me that I lived in one city, but worked in another. This was true. I lived in Edinburgh and commuted daily to an office in Glasgow. He informed me that I was a writer and that my home was full of many books and paintings, which it was. Next he told me that there was somebody important in my life called Jamie, and that it was his birthday the next week and I had forgotten it. This was also true. My nephew and godson is called Jamie, and when I looked at my diary I discovered his birthday was the following Tuesday.

All inconsequential enough, but then there was no way he could have known anything about me prior to my visit, let alone what I did for a living. I had only given him my Christian name, and I could have come from London or Peebles or Dublin, for all he knew. Reassuringly, he told me I could look forward to a long and prosperous life.

Subsequently I was to see Swein regularly. A simple, kindly soul, there were times when I came to the conclusion that even he must be in awe of his gift, or at least at odds with understanding it. Inevitably, some of the darker revelations must be hard for him to live with, and the one thing that he must never do, no matter how tempting it might be, he says, is meddle with fate.

Sometimes he tries to warn people if he believes the outcome to something he sees is uncertain, but he mostly avoids telling them anything that will distress them. He sees himself as a Christian and a force for good. He is not there to play God, but whether by chance or not, his powers of observation can be disturbing. On one occasion he sat next to the Wick-born painter Fionna Carlisle in an Edinburgh restaurant and told her that he saw visions of the sea and great sadness. Fionna's family tree, it transpired, includes the five widows of Clyth whose husbands were drowned in a herring boat off the Caithness coast in 1876.

The accident happened on 27 January 1876. Clyth is several miles south of Wick, and the boat was observed floating close inshore, not far from a dangerous skerry. She was speedily brought to land and it was found that whatever had been the cause of the accident, it must have happened as the boat was approaching the shore. The nets were in the boat, the sail was set, and it is believed that the crew had been rowing at the time the sea struck and swamped them. Entangled in the nets was the body of Thomas Sutherland, Fionna's great-great-grandfather, but all of the others were lost.

The body of Donald Sinclair was discovered later the same day. A diver from Wick, using diving equipment belonging to the British Fisheries Society, searched for the others some days later. He eventually found the body of William Mackay in about six and a half fathoms of water, lying on the edge of a rock. The Clyth Calamity Fund was set up locally to help the bereaved. Twenty-six children lost their fathers in the tragedy.

In the early 1980s, Swein and Isabelle came to Edinburgh regularly on visits and on one occasion, stayed with me at Douglas Crescent. At the time I was editor of *Scottish Field* magazine and one day the marketing department came up with the idea of holding a competition along the lines of the highly successful book, *The Hare*. In other words, it was to be a treasure hunt.

A sterling silver Quaich featuring candle-holders and decorated with amethysts was commissioned from the well-known designer Michael Laing, and the idea was that somewhere in Scotland a talisman would be hidden. The responsibility for this was given to Walt Unsworth, the Cumberland-based editor of the outdoors magazine *Climber & Rambler*, and each month he was asked to write a fictitious storyline providing hints to *Scottish Field* readers. It was my idea that

Swein be asked to launch the competition in Glasgow and write down on a piece of paper where he believed the talisman to be hidden. This was placed in a sealed container in the vaults of the Royal Bank of Scotland.

The launch event in June 1981 was a great success and the competition rambled on for several months until Sandy and Elspeth Hamilton from Edinburgh struck it lucky. The determined couple had made eight trips constantly referring to an Ordnance Survey map. The break came when they discovered an old road above a new road, beside which there was a rocky burn with a distinctive waterfall at its head. Climbing down the left bank, the Hamiltons came to a rock hollow with three trees. Across the burn was a small, pointed rock pinnacle. The talisman was hidden in a rock below the tree nearest the burn.

When Swein's prophesy was removed from the bank and read out, he had not only foreseen that the talisman would be found by a married couple from Edinburgh, but that it would be the wife who would direct the search. He had identified the hiding place as close to the Grey Mare's Tail, north of Moffat, but then had indicated a nearby graveyard. This was puzzling as there was no sign of a contemporary church to be seen, but then we found an ancient map of the area. Sure enough, there had been an old protestant church on the spot a hundred years earlier and the graveyard had disappeared under the subsequent grazing land.

Swein returned to Easter Ross in triumph. But then things became complicated. In 1984, he met Lindsay Mackinnon, a former nurse, and left Isabelle, who later found happiness when she married Ian E. Kaye, a former soldier and poet.

In 1992, I had a telephone call from Lindsay asking for help. Among the many visitors from all over the world that came to seek out Swein was Joseph Rael, otherwise known as Beautiful Painted Arrow of the Picuris Puebloe tribe of Red Indians. In his home in New Mexico, Beautiful Painted Arrow had had a vision of building a series of sacred chambers around the world in aid of peace. In his vision he had seen a circle of light and an angel carrying a child.

'Indian people are not allowed to analyze their own visions,' he explained to me when we met. 'I went at once to the elders of my tribe who agreed to excuse me from tribal duties for ten years so that I could make my dream a reality.'

Since then Beautiful Painted Arrow has written several cult best-sellers in America. In addition, he has supervised the building of chambers in twenty countries around the world. Every year, at each location, the people of the world are invited to take part in a three-day fast and sun dance, releasing their combined energies back into the atmosphere.

'Indians believe that the earth is our mother and that energy comes from the planets. When we dance, we release our tensions, and the energy we give off goes back into the stars,' he told me.

In a clearing in the woods behind the croft Lindsay had built a circular chamber with her own hands. At 6.30 a.m., the ancient ceremonial rites of the sun dance was started, with ritual chanting, and continued until 9 p.m. This was repeated over the remaining two days of the weekend. Followers came from as far afield as London and Devon. After this marathon dance session, Beautiful Painted Arrow departed for Vienna, travelling on to Norway and Australia.

Unfortunately, the administrative powers that be in Highland Region were not impressed. Shortly afterwards they demanded the chamber be pulled down on the pretext that the MacDonalds had not applied for planning permission to erect it in the first place.

Perhaps Swein should have seen this

coming, but no doubt it was too personal. Then again, perhaps it was meant to be. There was talk of new age travellers, and whispers of a hippy colony being set up, but as his reputation has grown, Swein has become used to the closed minds and opposition of those who seek to belittle him.

The mind, we know, is capable of remarkable feats. Many of its abilities we neither make use of nor are aware of. Yet if events can be willed, spoons bent, and inanimate objects moved through determined concentration, there seems no end to the power of the human spirit. It is as well that only a few among us are aware of our potential.

Swein MacDonald has located lost cats and dogs in London through talking to their owners over the telephone. He has directed distraught parents towards finding their run-away children. A classic example was when he was contacted by a couple in Lanarkshire whose teenage son had disappeared. After a few days, the police had been called in to help find him, but had informed the parents that it was too soon to be concerned. He was a difficult boy at a difficult age. There had been a family row, and the parents thought that he might have set off to see a friend who lived in Newcastle.

Swein thought otherwise. 'He is definitely not in Newcastle,' he told them. 'He is still in Scotland, with friends not far from here, and there are tall buildings around him. He is unharmed, except that he has hurt his shoulder. In two weeks' time he will grow tired of this and will either return or get in touch.'

Two weeks passed and much to the couple's relief, the lad turned up at a police station in Castlemilk asking to be taken home. As Swein had noted, he had strained his shoulder, but was disinclined to say how. Otherwise, he was in perfect health.

Even the police have been known to consult him over some of their more baffling cases, most notably that of a wealthy housewife who vanished without trace in the vicinity of Inverness. But probably the most alarming story in his casebook, told to me by Jane Durham, concerns two ladies who travelled to see him from Glasgow. Having given the first a reading, he explained to the second that he was exhausted and that his powers had deserted him. She was distraught, explaining that she had travelled two hundred miles to see him and that they had to return to Glasgow immediately afterwards. Still he declined.

She became agitated and tears came to her

eyes. Finally, he was persuaded, but no, he would not give her a reading. Instead, he agreed to write down a prophecy on a slip of paper to be placed in a sealed envelope, and she must promise that it would not be opened until she reached home.

The two ladies departed satisfied, the sealed envelope inserted safely into the driver's handbag. Tragically, just south of Drumochter, their car was involved in a head on crash with a lorry and the driver was killed. The passenger survived and much later, when she could bring herself to do so, she opened the handbag and extracted the envelope. Inside it she found a blank sheet of paper.

18

Madam Zara, Margaret Oliphant and Lady Nairne

Better lo'ed ye canna be,
Will ye no come back again?

Lady Nairne, 'Bonnie Charlie's now awa'

When she and her husband Johnny decided to set up their own small-scale commercial brewery in 2001, Tuggy Delap was determined that they should do so close to her childhood home at Cairndow, on the shores of Loch Fyne. Locating the brew house in an old farm steading, however, gave rise to unexpected complications. Shortly before their official opening in 2002, a bolt of lightning blew the modems of their computers, and a few weeks later, a substantial chunk of the distillery roof was completely blown off during a storm.

'It was as if we were jinxed,' says Tuggy who, having made a few enquiries, discovered that the former occupant of the farm had been a senior member of the Scottish

Temperance Society. 'That rather explained it, didn't it?' she says with an ironic chuckle.

Since the last incident, things have happily quietened down and the business is prospering. Fyne Ales is currently supplying and bottling their products (Pipers Gold, Maverick and Highlander) to select outlets, and the demand is growing. Johnny and Tuggy are sincerely hoping that the farm's previous occupant, having made his initial protest and announced his presence, is now content to let them get on with it.

When working for the *Daily Record* newspaper, Peter Samson, today a successful Glasgow-based public relations consultant, was instructed to interview Madam Zara, a white witch based at Kilchreggan in Argyll. At the time Peter was living in Falkirk in a house converted from a tied property, formerly a commercial tin manufacturing plant. 'As soon as I moved in, I wanted to move out,' he says.

Peter cannot explain exactly what it was about the place that disturbed him. It was a combination of different things. Sometimes there would be a lingering smell of stale tobacco in the dining room. Often it was as if somebody was moving about in the long L-shaped hallway. One night he recalls rushing to the front door thinking that somebody was trying to break in, but there

was nobody there. 'I'm not usually susceptible to that sort of thing,' he insists.

It was Madam Zara, however, who really
unnerved him. 'You're moving house,' she
told him when he called. 'You've never been
happy there, have you?'

It may have been simply guesswork, but
there was no way in which Madam Zara,
whom he had never met face to face, could
have known that his house was up for sale. 'A
word of warning,' she continued. 'Be careful
when you are packing because you will break
something of value. And when you leave,
close the door very quickly. You will feel much
happier then.'

Sure enough, when he was packing up the
contents of the house Peter dropped and
smashed a valuable ornament, but it had little
sentimental value. As he went out of the front
door for the last time, however, Madam
Zara's words came back to him. 'It was as if a
great weight was being lifted from my
shoulders,' he says. 'I slammed the door
behind me. Ridiculous, isn't it?'

Or is it?

The lodge was situated on a remote
peninsula of Wester Ross, and as soon as the
car turned into the long, pot-holed pathway
that masqueraded for a drive, Jan Watson, a
freelance caterer, knew that there was

something wrong. For a start there was the rubbish tip, or whatever it was, a mound of what looked like refuse in a clearing to the left, clearly visible from the car, where seagulls circled ominously like vultures. And then there was the vegetation on all sides, creeping and crawling as it encroached on the lodge itself, a bleak-looking place largely fabricated in timber. It looked as if it had been built in two halves. Or at least as if a substantial chunk of it had been added on as an afterthought.

The interior was equally gloomy, the timber construction causing the rooms to look dark at all times. The walls of the public rooms and the long corridors were lined with the heads of long dead stags with the dates of when they were shot inscribed on their mounts. Otherwise, there was little sign of any attempt at decoration. In the drawing room, the two large leather sofas were faded and split. The carpets were frayed, the floor boards scuffed, and despite the autumnal weather being relatively warm, there was a perpetual smell of damp.

Jan had signed up for a week to cook for a shooting house party at short notice. She had done this before, on the Island of Jura and in Sutherland. She normally brought a friend with her, but this time she was told that the house party comprised only six. It shouldn't be too difficult.

And certainly to begin with it proved not to be, except that from the moment she arrived, she hated the place. It wasn't her employers, an all-male group of shooting-made business executives, away from their wives but who showed little interest in her as a female. Besides, they were out for most of the day allowing her plenty of time to concentrate on and prepare the evening meals.

And it was not at night after everybody had gone to bed that she felt threatened. In fact, she fell asleep the moment her head touched the pillow. It was only in the afternoons that the walls closed in on her and she sensed she was being watched. Uncharacteristically, she expressed her concern to one of the house party and he told the others. They laughed. 'There's nobody around for miles,' she was informed.

To begin with, of course, there was nothing to become too worked up about. Items of shopping went missing. These involved nothing of value, only useful stuff such as flour and salt. Eggs, she had put aside for a soufflé were found broken and congealed on a stone shelf. Her handbag, which she was certain she had left in her bedroom, went missing and after a frantic search turned up

242

in the larder. The contents were intact, but Jan was unable to get rid of the suspicion that somebody had been going through them. 'I must be going insane,' she told herself.

Then it began to get nasty. She opened the bread tin she had filled only the previous day and it was crawling with maggots. There was no electricity at the lodge, which again she did not mind, but the antiquated coal-fired Aga was messy and repeatedly she found herself scrubbing the kitchen floor to remove a layer of soot dust that accumulated daily. Three days after her arrival she opened the hob and found an intact dead pigeon on top of the coals. How could that have got in there?

'It must have flown in by accident,' commented her employer unhelpfully when she showed it to him. Jan had rather liked him before that.

Often it would become very cold indoors despite the sun visibly shining outside through the windows. 'This is an unloved place,' Jan thought to herself, and shivered.

Towards the end of the week when she once again expressed concern over being left on her own, one of the guns generously agreed to leave his dog with her, a big old black Alsatian called Ben. 'Nobody will trifle with Ben, will they boy?' said the owner, giving the brute a pat on the back.

Jan looked at the beast and wondered if she might have felt safer without him. However, she accepted the offer, and for his part, Ben appeared perfectly happy to take on the role of guard dog. For a start it meant that he was permitted to sleep in a basket in the kitchen, away from the other dogs, who slept in outdoor kennels.

Every morning, rain or shine, after the men had set off with their picnic lunches, Jan drove to the village to pick up the newspapers and provisions. On the Friday, having decided to leave Ben behind at the lodge, she set off purposefully. Village stores, she knew, were the fount of all knowledge, and she was determined to find out who was the owner of the lodge and something about its history.

That did not help over much. It transpired that the lodge belonged to a syndicate and had done so since the 1970s. However, as she was leaving, the shopkeeper called her back. 'Talk to the postmistress,' he advised.

'Where do I find her?' asked Jan.

'In the back of the shop,' he said. 'She's my wife.'

From a desk in front of a window, the postmistress produced a file of old newspaper cuttings. Leafing through them, she handed Jan an article from a local paper dated 1968.

244

The headline spoke for itself. 'Stalker killed in shooting accident. Grandson drowns.'

In the matter-of-fact style of reportage of the period, the article went on to reveal that the man who had owned the lodge at the time, and who had been responsible for enlarging it, had been accidentally shot by his own grandson. The boy, tortured by what he had done, had not long after taken his own life by throwing himself off a rowing boat and into a loch.

'Can't say I ever knew any of them,' said the postmistress. 'Before our time, but I always thought that a dismal place when I've been up there. Can't think how anybody could stick staying there even if they are hell bent on killing some poor beast.'

Jan thanked her and set off. Half way up the pathway, she once more noticed the refuse tip and pulling over onto the verge, she left the car to walk over and have a look at it. As she did so, she again had the same feeling that she was being watched. When she reached the dump it was even more disgusting than she had imagined. What looked like a dead cow was lying on the top of it, the remains surrounded by seagulls that darted backwards and forwards and wheeled above her.

It was then that she realized that it was not

a cow at all, but a dog. It was Ben, the poor brute recruited to look after her. In a panic, Jan ran to the car, drove back to the village and went directly to the police station. A constable accompanied her back to the dump.

'He's poisoned himself,' said the policeman, sounding disappointed. 'He should never have been allowed near this place. Not fit for human beings, let alone pets.'

'Where on earth does all this garbage come from?' exclaimed Jan, almost hysterical.

'Folks around here just bring their rubbish here and dump it,' said the policeman. 'Nobody comes up this way much except the shooting tenants. It's not much of a beauty spot, is it?'

The official verdict on Ben was that he had choked on some polythene wrapping he had swallowed. Jan found this hard to believe, but was far more distraught about having to tell his owner that the dog was dead. Much to her amazement, he took it remarkably well. 'Silly old brute would tuck into anything in sight,' he said as he poured himself a Scotch. 'Serves him right.'

Jan prepared lunch for the group and tidied up the house the following morning. The shooting party set off in a hired bus in the afternoon, and the keys to the lodge were collected by a factor or some such person who turned up to see them off.

'Of all the places I have ever been on this planet that was the most unpleasant,' said Jan afterwards. 'I can't explain why. It was just horrid. Wild horses wouldn't drag me back there.'

Other homes, mercifully, have an entirely different ambience, welcoming and friendly, as if the previous occupants are determined to protect those who live within their walls. Such a place is Ardblair Castle, near Blairgowrie, which members of the Blair Oliphant family have occupied since the fourteenth century.

Laurence Blair Oliphant, the magnificently bearded twenty-third laird of Ardblair, has had no personal experience of ancestral sightings, but his wife Jenny, son Charles and daughters Amelia and Philippa are convinced that there are benign unseen forces protecting their interests and looking after their well being.

A Pictish settlement once stood here, surrounded on three sides by a loch. Positioned in a naturally protected area, today's castle, built on four sides of a courtyard, dates from the sixteenth century, and was erected on the site of a twelfth-century building. In some places the walls are ten feet thick, with the string of rooms and connecting passages adding to a sense of warmth and security. Nowadays, as in the past, it remains very much a family home, engaging the imagination from the moment you enter.

The last male heir of the Blair family died in the first half of the eighteenth century and Ardblair passed to his daughter Rachel, who had married Dr John Robertson of Edinburgh. They also had no son, but when their daughter married Laurence Oliphant, eighth Laird of Gask, he changed his surname to Blair Oliphant out of respect for his wife's ancestry.

The sixth and seventh lairds of Gask, both named Laurence, had been staunch Jacobite supporters, the latter an aide-de-camp to Prince Charles Edward Stuart. Both survived the Battle of Culloden to escape into exile abroad where they remained for seventeen years. The younger of the two never renounced his Jacobite sentiments and to his death refused to allow the names of the reigning Hanoverian monarchs to be mentioned in his presence.

Ardblair Castle is therefore filled with Jacobite memorabilia, notably Bonnie Prince Charlie's despatch box, his brogues, his gloves, white cockade, a competent drawing by the prince himself, and the Stuarts' light blue Order of the Garter ribbon, changed to dark blue by the Hanoverians, hence the expression 'True Blue.' The influence of 'The Kings Over The Water' prevails, but it is not they who are watching over the Blair Oliphant family.

The best known of the ghost stories of Ardblair, concerns Jean Drummond from nearby Newton Castle who in the sixteenth century, on hearing of the death of her fiancé, one of the Blair sons, drowned herself in the nearby River Ericht. Most of the sightings of Jean have taken place in the narrow passageway leading into the Long Gallery. Both Charles and Amelia have seen her, watched door handles turn, and sensed her footsteps following them. When Charles was very young, Laurence and Jenny came upon him sitting at the window in the Long Gallery staring intently at the lawn outside. When they asked him what had caught his attention, he replied, 'They're dancing. Look, they're dancing,' and went on to describe the small people he was watching on the grass below. Meanwhile, the family dogs had frozen on the lawn outside with their heads moving backwards and forwards watching something that only they and Charles could see.

One of the treasures of the house is a

life-size portrait of Margaret Oliphant by the artist John Watson Gordon, pupil of Sir Henry Raeburn. It was originally housed at Gask House, west of Perth, before being taken to Ravelston House in Edinburgh, and it was then kept in storage until Laurence brought it home to Ardblair.

Obviously this was a good move. Almost at once, old family documents and papers thought to have been lost began to re-appear in rooms where they had remained hidden for decades. Amelia remembers moving some of the other family portraits around to make room for the portrait of Margaret, and suddenly realizing that everything was fitting into place. 'It was as if she was saying to us that she approved,' she says. 'She was home where she belonged.'

Then just as they had finished re-hanging the pictures, quite astonishingly, a musical clock bought by Laurence's great-grandfather started up all on its own. 'It might have been caused by the vibration taking place with all of the moving around,' says Amelia. 'But it gave us all a terrible shock at the time.'

Amelia is currently preoccupied with writing a memoir of Carolina Oliphant of Gask, Margaret's sister, who is best known for her classic Scottish songs including 'The Hundred Pipers', 'Charlie is my Darling',

'The Laird of Cockpen' and 'Caller Herrin.' Born in 1766, Carolina married the fifth Lord Nairne in 1806, and under the pen-name of Mrs Brogan of Bogan, contributed lyrics to *The Scottish Minstrel*. A room at Ardblair is filled with items from her bedroom at Gask: her four-poster bed, piano, wedding veil and a piece of the pear tree from Gask under which she wrote 'The Auld Hoose.'

Over twenty years ago, Jimmy Black, a well-known radio and television broadcaster, came to the castle to make a programme focussing on the religious content of Lady Nairne's work. They set up their cameras and lights in the bedroom, but it became impossible to start recording because whenever a member of the family was not in the room, either the lights would fuse or the sound equipment would pack up. Both Laurence and Jenny were busy with household chores, so it was just not possible for them to be there all of the time and eventually it was decided to leave Charles, then only a baby, in the room. Thereafter nothing untoward happened, but only after Jimmy had shouted out in frustration, 'Carolina, would you no let me get on with it!'

As a new bride arriving at her husband's

ancestral home, Jenny Blair Oliphant was anxious to make an impression on the old house, and for it to accept her, although she insists that at the time she most certainly did not believe in ghosts. She would often sneak upstairs to Carolina's room to play the piano, and one afternoon decided that the backing material behind the fretwork, a piece of torn, dirty brown cloth, badly needed to be replaced. She told her husband about it and volunteered to re-upholster it if he could remove the fretwork.

He fetched his toolbox while downstairs, in a drawer, Jenny came across some fine, pale blue silk and immediately took it upstairs. There was just enough material to cut out the required two rectangles, but when Laurence showed her the fragments of old cloth he had removed from the piano, they were both astonished. Where the light had failed to touch the original fabric, the material was an exact match with the cloth she had found. 'It was then that I finally felt that the old house had accepted me,' she says.

The protective influence of the old house takes other turns. In the winter of 1981 to 1982, the overnight temperature in the central Highlands dropped as low as -17° centigrade. Jenny had taken the children to visit her parents in New Zealand and

Laurence had been left behind. Everything at Ardblair began to freeze up, even the supply pipe, until only a dribble of water was obtainable from the kitchen sink. The thaw began swiftly one February night, and Laurence suddenly woke up at 4 a.m. imagining that he had heard a voice shouting at him, 'Get up to the top of the house!'

Reluctantly getting out of bed and convinced he was having a bad dream, he had just reached the bottom of the staircase when the trickle of water began. 'If I hadn't gone upstairs and reached the pipe in time, the damage it would have caused would be unthinkable,' he says.

Some years later Jenny too had a similar experience on the night of their wedding anniversary. It was 11 August and she had told Laurence that they would be spending the night away. Unknown to him, she had pitched a large double tent on the lawn beside the house and furnished it with a mattress and bottles of champagne.

It was a fine, clear night, and the two of them shared a romantic dinner before retreating to their private pavilion to finish the champagne. Laurence, however, promptly fell fast asleep, and Jenny, who did not feel tired at all, decided to take the dogs for a walk in the moonlight. Having done so, she sat down on a stone on the front drive where she nodded off. Waking suddenly, she returned to the tent, but as she passed the back door she heard a pipe burst. Again, if there had not been anybody on hand to deal with it, the damage would have been substantial. Furthermore, water pipes do not usually burst on warm summer nights.

Ardblair Castle is situated in a particularly serene and scenically rich part of the Highland Perthshire landscape. The farmland is plentiful. This is the heart of berry-picking country where the hills and glens undulate gently across the horizon. Every September, the Blairgowrie Highland Games, held in the Bogle Field at Ardblair, is a major visitor attraction rivalling the better known Royal Braemar Gathering held the previous day some thirty miles to the north. Laurence, needless to say, is Games Chieftain. Spectators who have never seen cabers tossed or shots put are enthralled by the goings on.

On a summer afternoon in 1951, Laurence was walking down to some trees on the edge of a wood when a huge animal suddenly crossed his path, right to left. He was astonished at its size, but even more so by the speed with which it disappeared. 'It had enormous antlers and was totally silent,' he says. 'I wasn't scared by it, only startled, and I had no idea what it was.'

Laurence did not mention the encounter to anybody, but exactly thirty years later Jenny, walking in the same wood, had exactly the same experience. 'It came out of nowhere and ran in front of me, right to left,' she says. 'At first, I thought it must be a deer, but it was far too big. It never occurred to me that it might have been a phantom until one night we were watching a television programme about a large beast found in Ireland, an Irish Elk. Both Laurence and I instantly recognized it as the same animal we had seen in the woods, but what was even more intriguing is that it was an extinct species.'

It might sound absurd and totally self-indulgent for me even to mention it, but on the Monday following my visit to Ardblair I found myself thirty miles north-west of Blairgowrie at a banquet hosted at Blair Castle, in Blair Atholl, by the Keepers of the Quaich, the exclusive society formed by companies within the Scotch whisky industry. At this we were entertained by the distinguished Scottish musical group Ceol Alba, featuring harp, fiddle, flute, bass and piano. Given my recent inspection of her personal belongings, was it only coincidence that the selection of songs they played that night all originated from the pen of Lady Nairne?

19

The Small People

In Screapadale of my people,
where Norman and Big Hector were,
their daughters and their sons are a
   wood
going up beside the stream.

               Sorley Maclean,
'Time, the deer, is in the wood of Hallaig'

Sandy Scott, sales executive for Praban na Linne, the Gaelic Whiskies, was on a fishing trip to Loch Hope, close to Altnaharra in Sutherland, and his ghillie was a local man, Murdo Sutherland. The day dawned with a beautiful southerly breeze creating a perfect ripple on the water. It was 9 a.m. when they set off in the boat and at exactly 10 a.m. Sandy noticed a variation on the loch surface.

Instantly a perfect grilse was hooked and after twenty minutes' play, it was landed. Having given it the last rites, Murdo weighed it and announced that it was exactly 5lb 3oz. Naturally Sandy was delighted, but even more so when having made his next cast, he noticed a similar ripple on the surface. Once again it took him exactly twenty minutes to reel in his second catch.

'It's another beautiful cock fish, Mr Scott,' said Murdo, placing the two fish side by side. 'Look at them. They're identical twins.'

At this point, said Sandy, an extraordinary feeling of precognition came over him and he said to Murdo, 'And I can tell you how much it will weigh — 5lb 10oz.'

'You'll be guessing, Mr Scott,' said Murdo, but sure enough the second fish weighed exactly 5lb 10oz.

Murdo was impressed. 'How on earth would you be knowing that?' he asked.

Sandy shook his head. 'On 4 February 1940 my wife gave birth to twin boys. One weighed 5lb 3oz and the other, 5lb 10oz.'

Murdo stared at him and said, 'The fairies are about. We'll catch no more fish today.' Within minutes a brisk wind blew up from the north causing white horses to canter across the loch. 'And you've had no more children since then,' observed Murdo. Sandy and his wife had divorced, but there was no way Murdo could have known this, so Sandy asked him what had given him that impression.

Murdo simply tapped his nose with a

forefinger and said: 'The fairies told me.'

Fairies crop up throughout Scottish folk-lore, but tend to predominate in the Highlands. Their cultural origin in the British Isles is to a great extent Celtic Irish. However, like all the organic growths of nature or of fancy, fairies are not the immediate product of one country or, indeed, of one time. Similar beings were said to exist in Palestine and Greece under different names, and in England there are dwarfs, pixies and brownies. In Scandinavia there are trolls. Robert Louis Stevenson discovered that a belief in lady fairies, deathly to human lovers, was as common in Samoa as it was in Strathfinlas and on the banks of Loch Awe.

In essence, therefore, fairies are the spirits of the dead gathered together in remote places, hills and forests, around lakes and river banks, away from human kind. Primitive people, such as the Dyaks of Borneo, among whom I was born, or the Aboriginees in Australia, retain similar beliefs about the spirits of their ancestors.

The fairy changeling belief was once commonplace in Argyll, and a fairy boy dwelt long in a small farmhouse in Glencoe, now unoccupied. In Glencoe there is also a fairy hill where locals claim that music, vocal and instrumental, can be heard in still weather.

Schiehallion, on nearby Rannoch Moor, is the fairy mountain. On the Black Isle, notably at the side of the A832, 5½ miles from Inverness and in Aberdeenshire, Argyll and Angus, there are Cloutie Wells where rags and shreds of clothing are tied to the branches of surrounding trees and bushes as offerings to the little people.

In this day and age it is not surprising that people are largely reluctant to step forward and admit to believing in fairies, but at the risk of being ridiculed it is intriguing to discover that there are those who most certainly do. And those that do have a very different interpretation as to who or what these creatures are to the popular conception. Scots literature owes most of what it knows on the subject to the Revd Robert Kirk, minister of Aberfoyle in the seventeenth century, a seventh son who penned *The Secret-Commonwealth*, an impressive treatise which two centuries after the author's death made such an impression on Sir Walter Scott that he published a limited edition of the manuscript for his own enjoyment.

The reality is that in the Scottish oral tradition, fairies were a long ago pigmy people who lived in subterranean earth-houses, and to explore this theory further all roads inevitably lead to the Isle of Skye where there are Fairy Pools in Glen Brittle, overlooked by the Cuillin Mountains and, on the west coast, a Fairy Glen, close to Balnaknock which features no less than 365 grassy hillocks, some 115 feet high. There are many places on Skye named after the fairies — 'na Sithein.' Sith is a fairy and curiously the same word means 'peace.'

There are several traditions associated with the Fairy Flag kept at Dunvegan Castle, ancestral stronghold of Clan MacLeod who are of Norse origin.

The Norse Sagas suggest that it was first acquired by Harald Hardvarder who led an invasion to the Holy Land and came back with much wealth and the flag which, whenever it was unfurled, guaranteed him victory in battle. Harald invaded England several years before his nephew William the Conqueror did so, but Harold of England made a rapid march to Stamford Bridge and attacked the Norse army as it slept. The flag had been left on one of the longboats and 'before they could fetch the flag, the battle was lost'.

Presumably somebody had been sent to fetch the flag, missed the battle and went off with the flag. All the Norsemen were killed with the exception of the flag party. Did they flee to the Isle of Man? Was the flag used by the invading Vikings at Largs two centuries later?

Did the Norse leader King Haakon try to persuade the MacLeod Chief (by now Gaelicized) to join forces with him? Or did he end up with the flag of his Norse relations and did not dare to admit where it had come from? So he put it about that a fairy had flown through a window into the nursery at Dunvegan and wrapped the infant chief, asleep in his cot, in the mystical flag while singing a fairy lullaby to him.

Whichever story, if either, is correct, the provenance of the flag on display in a glass case at the castle has been surrounded with magical powers ever since its arrival. Unfortunately, its strength is believed to be limited, and according to the piper and writer Seton Gordon, the three occasions for which it was said it would hold its enchantment were used up long ago.

Gordon, whom I was fortunate enough to visit at his home at Duntulm in the north of Skye before his death in 1977, spoke of it first being unfurled at the Battle of Glendale around the year 1490, and at the Battle of Trumpan at Vaternish in 1580. On each occasion, MacLeod was triumphant. However, according to Gordon, the third and last occasion on which the Fairy Flag was unfurled was a disastrous, but astonishing, fulfilment of a prophecy made in the seventeenth century by Coinneach Odhar, the Brahan Seer.

When Norman (son) of the Third Norman, the son of the slender, bony, English lady, should die by accidental death; when MacLeod's Maidens should become the property of a Campbell; when a fox should have her young in one of the turrets of the castle; and when the Fairy Flag should be taken out of its box for the third and last time and unfurled, then the Glory of the MacLeods should depart, a great part of their land would be sold, and a curach or coracle would be large enough to carry all the tacksmen of the name of MacLeod across the sea loch. But in later times a MacLeod named Iain Breac would arise who would redeem the estates and would raise the power and honour of the house of MacLeod to a high degree.

The fulfilment of all but the last part of this did indeed come to pass in 1799 when an English smith staying at Dunvegan, and the MacLeod's business manager, secretly broke into the iron chest in which the flag was kept for safekeeping. By exposing the flag for the third time, Gordon was convinced that they had destroyed its potency.

Almost at once came the news that Norman, son of the third Norman, had been blown up in HMS *Queen Charlotte* while serving as a lieutenant in the Navy. Not long after, the property of Orbost, upon which the rocks known as MacLeod's Maidens are situated, was sold to Angus Campbell of Ensay. Then a tame fox that had been adopted by the same Norman, son of the third Norman, was discovered to have had a litter of cubs in the west turret of the castle.

At the time the prophecy was made, there were more than thirty tacksmen of the name of MacLeod on the estate. Not one remains today. Before the First World War there were hopes that Iain Breac, son of Canon Rory MacLeod of MacLeod would fulfil the concluding part of the prophecy, but he was killed and there remained no male heir in direct descent.

The MacLeod chiefship thereafter passed through the female line to the current chief John MacLeod of MacLeod, who stirred up a considerable amount of controversy when he put the Cuillin Mountains up for sale to raise money for re-roofing Dunvegan Castle. Perhaps it is impertinent to suggest that at least one of his grandchildren or great-grandchildren be christened Iain Breac.

In their comprehensive book *Scottish Fairy Belief*, Lizanne Henderson and Edward J. Cowan, Professor of Scottish History at Glasgow University, observe that it was religious impetus, both protestant and catholic, that subjected the fairies to a process of demonization. 'Such was the climate of suppression and persecution that it is often difficult to understand how fairy belief survived relatively unscathed, if somewhat refurbished and sanitized, into the modern era.'

In *A Description of the Western Isles of Scotland*, the early travel writer Martin Martin indicates that fairy belief was widespread throughout the Hebrides, singling out Lewis, Colonsay and Benbecula. Off the north-west coast of Lewis is the island of Luchruban, said to have been inhabited long ago by pigmy folk. Martin calls it 'The Island of the Little Men,' and records that small bones resembling human bones were found here.

Merchant banker Sir Iain Noble, founder of Skye's Gaelic College Sabhal Ostaig Mor, has no doubts that the fairies once existed. 'They were the people who lived here in the islands long, long ago. They were driven out of their original homes onto poorer land by the incomers and possibly through diet and interbreeding, they just got smaller. They had their own language, religion and their own customs and they kept their distance from those who were not of their own kind, but who needed their help at harvest time. They may well have been the original Pictish people for all we know of them.'

On a bright February afternoon Sir Iain and Lady Noble took me to visit one of the six fairy houses in Gleann an Uird on Sleat in the south-east of Skye. On our journey we passed Loch na Bhraichean, the Loch of Shadows, where a water horse is said to hold dominion. At one stage it was decided to drag the loch in an attempt to capture it, whatever it was, but when the net was cast something heavy pulled it deep down into the water and the ambitious fishermen ran away in terror. The net is still there to this day.

Approximately half way through Gleann an Uird, our vehicle was abandoned and our adventure continued on foot, steeply up a hillside to a plateau below a cliff top whereupon sat the fairy house. This curious circular habitat, I was informed, dates from around 2000 BC, measures approximately 20 feet across, with 2 feet walls, and was originally roofed with turf supported by posts so as to be below the ground. Two have recently been archaeologically excavated by Historic Scotland working with Roger Miket, the Museums Officer in Portree, and an English professor of archaeology.

'They told me they had no prior knowledge of people living in round houses from that period,' said Sir Iain, and when he suggested that perhaps it was where the fairies had lived, they looked at him in astonishment.

'They were unaware of the Highland oral tradition,' he explained. 'They thought I meant fairies with wings, the way the Victorians imagined them. I had to explain that I was referring to 'the people who lived here before.' These people were pushed off all the best ground by incomers, possibly the Scots from Ireland, but not too far off because they were needed every year to help out with the harvest.'

According to Sir Iain, they always remained on the fringe of good arable ground, hence the extraordinary remains of the round house we visited under a rock face high on an exposed hillside with distant views of snow-capped Beinn Sgritheal and the Saddle, the mountains above Loch Hourne, on the Scottish mainland. Strategically the four thousand-year-old fairy homestead with its stone centre fireplace and front entrance facing east could not have been better placed since any people coming to visit them would have been spotted long before their arrival.

Momentarily silent, we stood and marvelled at the view, as others must have done for centuries before us. After the heavy rain of the night before, the landscape sparkled. There was not a soul in sight, yet a sense that we too were being watched. 'When I first went for a walk along Allt an Leth-Sithein, the wooded stream that runs into Gleann an Uird, I was certain I was being followed' said Lady Noble. 'I couldn't see anybody. I just had this feeling that I was not alone, that there were eyes in the trees all around me.'

When she told her husband about this later he told her that Allt an Leth-Sithhein in Gaelic means 'Burn of the half-fairy.'

Do not doubt it, we are rarely, if ever, entirely alone upon this earth.

20

Premonitions

Let what can be shaken, be shaken,
And the unshakeable remain.
The Inaccessible Pinnacle is not
  inaccessible.

Hugh MacDiarmid (C.M. Grieve),
'The Happy Poet'

When she lived in Edinburgh during the
1990s, Marion Bowles, a freelance relief
cook, took a weekend job working at a
modern nursing home in Corstorphine.
'Unfortunately, it wasn't one of those
hospitals where you ever got to know people,'
she recalled. 'It was all relatively formal and
impersonal.'

This made it all the more difficult when,
looking out of the hospital windows in the
afternoons, she began to see figures in the
hospital garden of a definite sex and hair
colour, and would, on the next shift, discover
that somebody fitting the exact same
description had since died. 'I noticed them to

begin with because the garden was off-limits to the patients and I wondered what they were doing there,' she said. 'What made it worse was that there was nobody there that I could talk to about it. They would have thought I was bonkers.'

Marion has had premonitions since she was a child, but usually only when her life is progressing on an even keel. Often, when the telephone rings, she says, she knows in advance who it will be. Normally this does not bother her. However, three months at the nursing home was as much as she could take, and she handed in her notice.

To some extent, the family fortunes of the distinguished Noble family of Argyll began in Greenock, where one of their number married a lady whose father had emigrated to Virginia in the Carolinas with his wife and two children. In due course, the wife had died and the children were despatched home to Greenock where they lived with their maiden aunt.

Under such circumstances, the brother and sister became close, so it was a major heartbreak when, having reached a certain age, a summons came for the son to join his father in America. Time passed and the sister became engaged to a young man called Noble, and wrote immediately to her brother asking him to attend the wedding.

There was no reply, but shortly before the big day she was seated in a downstairs room while her aunt combed out her hair. Suddenly she said: 'Look Aunt, George has arrived.'

'Where?' asked her aunt.

'There, through that door,' she said. 'He came in and went out again.'

Immediately they sent to the harbour for news, only to be told that no ship had arrived from the Virginias. The girl, however, was certain that she had seen her brother and fearing that something terrible had befallen him, she wrote the time and date of the sighting on a piece of paper and placed it on the mantelpiece.

Alas, her brother did not appear for the wedding, but arrived on the doorstep two months afterwards full of apologies. He had received her summons but been unable to respond. Then he told her how one night he had had a dream in which he found himself outside the Greenock house and, walking through a door, had seen her and their aunt in a downstairs room. Her hair was being combed.

'When I woke up I was terrified that something had happened to you,' he told her. 'That was when I resolved that even though I had missed your wedding, I had to come back to see if you were all right.'

Examples of the bonds within families are legion, especially the sensitivities shared by identical twins.

As a dietary expert, Marion Bowles was consulted by two identical sisters both suffering from ME, one of whom suffered from severe food allergies. 'The curious aspect of it was that when one twin ate either chicken or banana, the other would have the reaction,' said Marion. 'Her lips would swell up and she'd rush to the telephone to accuse her sister.'

Throughout their lives identical sisters Zandra and Zoe Hall from Stanley in Perthshire have shared similar responses. When Zoe's appendix flared up and she was rushed into hospital, Zandra was on her way home from Edinburgh and felt her pain. 'I can't begin to explain why I did it, but I went straight to Perth Royal Infirmary and walked into the ward where Zoe had been taken,' she said afterwards.

A similar story concerns the mother who was just setting off to the cinema with her teenage son and as they were going out of the front door, they heard the telephone ringing in the hall. The son was anxious to press on, so told his mother to ignore it. 'No,

271

something has happened to your sister,' she said, and rushed back into the house. Sure enough, there had been a motor scooter accident and the girl had been taken to a hospital.

On the death of his step-father in November 1987, Adrian Shaw, a languages student at Heriot Watt University in Edinburgh, was summoned home from his placement year in Paris. Following the funeral, he paid a courtesy call on a neighbour, a seventh child of a seventh child, known to have powers of second sight, who had, on a previous visit, inadvertently foretold his step-father's death. As is so often the case, what she had said at the time had not made sense. It made immediate sense when the event took place.

Employing a tea cup, the lady informed Adrian that although he was scheduled to return to Paris via Heathrow Airport the following morning, he would break his journey to meet up with an old friend in London, somebody he had not seen for a very long time.

This seemed improbable, but Adrian went along with it. 'You have no plans to do so at present,' she told him. 'But when you see a broken ring of diamonds you will know that this is what you must do,' she told him.

To convince him of this, she showed him the teacup, at the bottom of which was a circle of ten tea leaves. As she did so, the telephone rang in the hall. 'It's for you, Adrian,' called out the lady's daughter.

The overhead light had fused, so the hall was in darkness. The long distance telephone call, as it turned out, had been re-directed from next door where they had known where he was. Astonished, Adrian recognized the caller as a long lost childhood friend, now living in London. He had heard that Adrian's step-father had died and wanted the two of them to meet up, if possible, on Adrian's journey back to Paris.

At that same moment Adrian noticed the illuminated dial of the old fashioned telephone. The circle of ten digits, strongly visible in the dark, bore an unmistakable resemblance to a broken ring of diamonds.

As he took his farewell of the neighbour, she asked him what his plans were for that Christmas. Would he be coming home again?

Possibly not, he thought, considering how close it was, and the cost of having had to come back this time. 'You'll be back,' she said.

In the week before Christmas, Adrian's father died. Adrian once again came home for the funeral and afterwards dropped in to see the same neighbour. 'I knew something bad was going to happen when I saw you last,' she told him. 'But I couldn't be sure if it would be you or your father.'

Stewart Conn, who has been officially appointed Edinburgh's Makar or 'Poet Laureate' tells the story of a sensitive musician friend and his wife whose only son was the centre point of their lives. As a family they were unusually close, and one night the father had a dream in which he was holding his favourite guitar when its neck suddenly snapped and the strings fell loose. He later told his wife about this, and shortly afterwards their son came to visit them. 'I had an extraordinary dream a couple of nights ago,' he told them. 'I was holding a guitar when the neck suddenly broke.'

Stewart does not have a follow-up incident to give meaning to this disclosure, and to his knowledge all members of the family are well. What it does illustrate, however, is yet again how thought transfer between close individuals, particularly in dreams, is relatively commonplace.

The mind is an extraordinary implement, especially when influenced by emotional loyalties. The telepathic potential between each and every one of us is virtually unexplored. The belief that somehow everything in this existence is pre-ordained is not necessarily as daft as it sounds. How many of us make use of even a fraction of the senses that we are told that we have? Even the Bible refers to dreams as a pathway for revelation.

Dreams are our most potent channel of precognition, at their most vivid as we slip into the subconscious state of sleep or as we embark upon the process of waking up. These are the moments when we remember the most.

What takes place in our subconscious minds while we are in our deepest state of slumber nobody has ever been able to penetrate. We should therefore never dismiss dreams as aberrations. Too often they have been proved to be disturbingly accurate.

Dr Robert Marchant Wink, a general practitioner in Edinburgh, was called to the bedside of one of his patients in a hospital who told him that she wanted to thank him for what he had done for her before she died. She had been seriously ill, but there was reason to believe that she would not recover.

She thought not, however. 'I had a dream this morning, and it was the same dream that I have had several times before,' she told him. 'Always when I have it, somebody dies, and I know that this time it is my turn.'

She went on to describe how she had dreamt she was in a hallway where there was a longcase clock and a black dog. 'The clock showed 6 a.m. in the morning,' she said. 'That's when I will die.'

Making the appropriate gestures, Robert returned home that night. In the morning he had a telephone call from the hospital at 6.15 a.m. to inform him that his patient had died exactly as she herself had predicted, on the hour.

Simon Halliday is an Australian who moved to Glasgow ten years ago by chance. He had come to London from Sydney to look for work. His parents had emigrated when he was two years old, and he had wanted to see what the old country was like.

In fact, his parents had lived in Manchester, but his father had a brother in the hotel business in Glasgow, and it was the promise of a job that brought the twenty-two-year-old to Scotland. 'The weirdest thing was that as soon as I saw my uncle's hotel, I recognized it immediately. It was just so incredibly familiar.'

For years Simon had been having a recurring dream which made no sense to him. He saw himself in a hallway with a reception desk, and a corridor through to the back. On his right was a spacious lounge in which there were people sitting and talking. To the left was a glass partition behind which there were tables and chairs, in other words a dining room. He even recognized the tartan carpet.

In front of the hotel was a wide street along which the traffic was incessant. What had made the dream memorable, but disturbing, was that in it Simon had seen himself standing at the reception desk when a small child had broken away from his parents to run past him through the vestibule entrance and out onto the street outside. There had been a screech of brakes and a small thud, and Simon had rushed into the street to find the small boy crushed beneath the wheels of a car.

'It was ridiculous,' says Simon. 'Except that the dream was so incredibly vivid and it was always the same.'

Simon had been at the hotel less that a fortnight when a family with a small child booked in. He immediately recognized the little boy and decided to keep an eye on him. Then just before midday, it happened, just as he had dreamt it would.

The child, Simon concluded, was a spoiled brat, much indulged by his doting parents, and for once was obviously not getting his own way. Just as it had occurred in the dream, the kid broke away from his mother and ran towards the front door whereupon Simon dived across the hallway and tackled him, causing the boy to fall flat on his face.

'Of course the mother went hysterical,' says Simon. 'She called me every name under the sun and accused me of being a child molester.'

Meanwhile, the boy, momentarily stunned, was throwing another tantrum and the hotel manager was summoned.

Simon explained himself without mentioning the dream, and the manager complimented Simon on having done the right thing. The road was in fact notorious for people being run over. However, he cautioned Simon to keep his distance from the child's parents who in the meantime had gone ballistic and, until they eventually calmed down, were threatening to call the police.

'It just shows you, doesn't it?' reflects Simon. 'It really doesn't pay to interfere with fate.'

A lady who has specifically asked for her name not to be published in this book had a rather more far-reaching, if equally unsettling, experience of the kind. Not so very long ago she vividly recalls dreaming of an elderly family friend, a bachelor, who visited her bedside during the night to say goodbye. He was in London and she lived in Lanarkshire. It was an odd visitation since she had only known him as a friend of her parents. The following afternoon there was a telephone call from his housekeeper to say that he had died in his sleep.

In the same dream the old man had told her that he had written her a letter, but that it had not been posted. A few days before the funeral she was contacted by the deceased's lawyer and told that a letter had indeed been found. It had been written on the day of the old man's death and in it she was informed that he was her father, that her mother and the man whom she had always thought of as her father, were the only others who had known about this.

For the sake of her mother's marriage and reputation it had been agreed to keep the truth a secret until such time as it was thought appropriate to tell her. Both her mother and stepfather had died some years previously and carried the secret with them to their graves. Only the old man whom she had known as 'Uncle Jack' had felt, no doubt for selfish reasons, that it was important for her to know.

All of a sudden she became aware of Uncle Jack featuring regularly in old family photograph albums. She remembered the string of pearls he had given her on her eighteenth birthday, and the diamond earrings for her twenty-first. 'Nobody else to spend his money on,' her grandmother had commented sourly at the time.

As one can imagine, the revelation came as a thunderbolt out of the blue to this lady who had never had even the slightest suspicion of any irregularity in her parents' long and, by all appearances, happy marriage. The reality as it dawned upon her was somewhat cushioned, however, by her inheritance of the not inconsiderable bulk of Uncle Jack's fortune, with a few hundred acres of the far north of Scotland thrown in for good measure.

Absolution

He saw each separate height, each
vaguer hue,
Where the massed islands rolled in mist
away,
Though all ran together in his view
He knew that unseen straits between
them lay.

Edwin Muir, 'Childhood'

The obvious reason for most of us to believe
in a parallel universe of the spirits is because
we want to. You have to be very strong
minded and very disillusioned with existence
to believe that death is our ultimate end, that
when the heart stops beating there is nothing
more. Our very conceit of ourselves cries out
in protest. We are each and every one of us
the centre of an individual universe, obsessed
with our unique sense of self. When the lights
go out we must surely move on to somewhere
else. Otherwise what are we doing here in the
first place? There has to be an ongoing
purpose for us in the greater scheme of
things.

It is the presence of the inexplicable that gives us hope of an afterlife. It provides us with an answer to the inevitability of death. Religions of all kinds — Christian, monotheistic, polytheistic, philosophical and pagan — have mercilessly capitalized on this to their benefit and detriment.

So if an other-world awareness can comfort us, and in doing so if our senses can open us up to the unknown to help us find some meaning in our uncertainty, all to the good.

But, of course, what we are dealing with here is not exactly unknown. We are talking about beliefs that have been around since the dawn of mankind. The spirit world has been pondered over, dismissed and persecuted since our ancestors first began to acquire knowledge, and even now, when we can identify DNA and propel rockets into galaxies as yet undiscovered, we are no further forward in our understanding of shadows.

In Scotland there are those who, after 1,400 years of established Christianity, still mourn the demise of certain aspects of the old idolatories. Who can deny that our Druid ancestors were more circumspect in their rituals, more enchanted in the eyes of the beholder? Such as we know of them is bound up in a mysticism that still fascinates us, even if we cannot bring ourselves to endorse it.

More in harmony with nature than we could ever hope to be, who is to say that the ancient Celts were not closer to their own gods than we are to our God? How is it that we can date their antiquity, but are still at a loss to explain a purpose for the Ring of Brodgar on Orkney or the standing stones at Callanish on Lewis?

There are those who insist it is to do with sun worship; others that their very existence is a ground plan for the universe. Nobody to date has had anything much more positive to offer on the subject than blind speculation.

So what, if anything, has either Callanish or the Ring of Brodgar to do with the supernatural?

Long before the Scottish comedian Billy Connolly made humorous capital from dancing naked around the stones of Brodgar on camera, I was there to watch a sunrise. I was on Mainland to write about the islands. The weather was mild, and although it involved my getting out of bed at around 5 a.m., it seemed like a good idea at the time.

And spiritually, I can confirm that it was. I can think of nothing more sublimely beautiful than watching the golden first flush of day in that raw and extraordinary landscape of jagged columns, surrounded by the great silence of 5,000 years.

I was not there for the summer solstice or any symbolic or significant reason other than my just wanting to be there. Standing in the centre of the Temple of the Moon under that big sky, with no other human presence anywhere to be seen or heard, the past, the present, and the future seamlessly merged into one and the same.

I thought about this when the Revd Charles Robertson of the Canongate Kirk said to me: 'There is no *now* and *then*, only *now*. Time and place belong to the eternal here and now, and we dip in and out of them constantly.'

In the panic of city survival, there is little time or encouragement for us to reflect upon anything so patently self-indulgent as time travel. Only in the big open spaces such as on Orkney and on Lewis, where land meets sky and sky meets ocean, does it strike a chord. At Callanish, like Brodgar, the past is more potently present than anywhere else I know.

As with the spirits of the Small People on Skye, A.J. Stewart's realization that she was here before, the curses and the talismans of centuries past, and the manifold examples of the occult supplied by contributors from all walks of life, there has to be something going on.

If there is anything that I hope that this book might achieve, it is that readers may become more open to the possibilities of the worlds they inhabit.

We do hope that you have enjoyed reading this large print book.

Did you know that all of our titles are available for purchase?

We publish a wide range of high quality large print books including:
Romances, Mysteries, Classics
General Fiction
Non Fiction and Westerns

Special interest titles available in large print are:
The Little Oxford Dictionary
Music Book
Song Book
Hymn Book
Service Book

Also available from us courtesy of Oxford University Press:
Young Readers' Dictionary
(large print edition)
Young Readers' Thesaurus
(large print edition)

For further information or a free brochure, please contact us at:
Ulverscroft Large Print Books Ltd.,
The Green, Bradgate Road, Anstey,
Leicester, LE7 7FU, England.
Tel: (00 44) 0116 236 4325
Fax: (00 44) 0116 234 0205